TAYLOR'S WEEKEND GARDENING GUIDES

Barbara Ellis, Editor

Frances Tenenbaum, Series Editor

HOUGHTON MIFFLIN COMPANY

Boston • New York   1998

Easy Plant Propagation

Filling your garden with plants from seeds, cuttings, divisions, and layers

NANCY J. ONDRA

For information about permission to reproduce selections from this book,
write to Permissions, Houghton Mifflin Company, 215 Park Avenue South,
New York, New York 10003.

Taylor's Guide is a registered trademark of Houghton Mifflin Company.

Library of Congress Cataloging-in-Publication Data

Ondra, Nancy J.
    Easy plant propagation : filling your garden with plants from seeds, cuttings,
divisions, and layers / Nancy Ondra.
        p. cm. — (Taylor's weekend gardening guides)
    Includes index.
    ISBN 0-395-86295-7
    1. Plant propagation. 2. Gardening. I. Title. II. Series.
SB119.054 1998
635.9´153 — dc21   97-39672
                                                          CIP

Printed in the United States of America.

WCT 10 9 8 7 6 5 4 3 2 1

Book design by Deborah Fillion
Cover photograph © by Derek Fell

CONTENTS

The desire to learn about propagation is the mark of a true gardener. Maybe you're tired of the common plants for sale at your local garden center, and you want to try raising some more interesting ones from seed. Or perhaps you have already collected some particularly special plants that you'd like to share with your gardening friends by rooting cuttings or making divisions. Or maybe you just feel that you can't ever have enough plants, and propagating them yourself is the best way to fill your garden while staying within your budget.

Whatever your reason, propagation is a fun and rewarding aspect of gardening. Best of all, it's easy to get started. The secrets to successful propagation are simple: gather a few basic materials, choose the best technique for the plant you want to propagate, and provide good care to help your new plants grow and thrive.

Simple propagation practices make it easy and inexpensive to fill a garden with flowers. The annuals in this cottage garden are easily propagated from seed, and the rose is a shrub that can be propagated from cuttings.

Chapter 1
Getting Started

To get started with propagation, you don't need to invest in expensive or complicated equipment. You can find everything you need at your local garden center or in the gardening department of nearly every home-improvement center. If you don't have access to local sources, check your collection of seed and nursery catalogs. Start with the basics: a few different sizes of plastic pots, a few trays to hold the pots, and two or three kinds of growing medium.

Stock Up on Containers

While some propagation techniques don't require containers, you will need them for most methods. Suitable containers can include anything that will hold seed-starting mix, potting soil, or some other growing medium. Of course, some containers work better than others. It's true you can come up with all kinds of homemade containers, including egg cartons, cut-down milk cartons, margarine

To propagate and grow lots of plants quickly and easily, create a nursery bed that is similar to, but smaller than, this commercial planting filled with phlox, irises, hostas, and other shade-loving plants. Choose a site in sun or shade depending on what you'd like to grow, and dig in plenty of organic matter to provide rich, well-drained soil.

containers, Styrofoam cups, and other recycled materials — anything that's at least 1 inch deep and that you can punch drainage holes in. But for consistent results, you're better off starting with commercially made containers — either purchased or recycled. Commercially made pots are uniform in size, so they tend to dry out evenly, making watering easier. With a collection of homemade containers, some will dry out sooner than others, so you'll have to check them more often and water much more carefully. If your space is limited, you'll also appreciate the way commercial containers tend to fit together snugly, unlike an assortment of cups and cartons.

If you've been gardening for any length of time, chances are you already have a collection of plastic pots and flats (those shallow trays that hold a dozen or more pots). You may also have kept the market packs (molded plastic inserts, usually with four or six "cells") that most annual and vegetable transplants are sold in. You can reuse any of these materials for your propagation projects. It's best to rinse them out before using them, or at least brush out any clinging soil. Some gardeners prefer to "sterilize" containers before reuse, by dipping them into a 10 percent bleach solution (one part household bleach to nine parts water). But many busy gardeners don't bother with this step, unless they've had problems with diseases attacking their seedlings or cuttings in the past. With a little care, you can reuse plastic containers for many years.

If you didn't happen to keep any pots, flats, or packs from previous plantings, you're still in luck: it's generally quite easy to find them for sale in a range of sizes. Here's a rundown of the most commonly available containers, and their suggested uses:

$2\frac{1}{2}$-**inch pots:** for starting small quantities of small seeds or individual large seeds; also good for potting up small, newly rooted cuttings.

$3\frac{1}{2}$-**inch pots:** for starting moderate quantities of small, medium, or large seeds; also useful for potting up individual rooted cuttings or larger seedlings.

4-inch pots: for starting larger quantities of small, medium, or large seeds; ideal for rooting multiple cuttings, for potting up large individual cuttings or seedlings, or for potting up small divisions.

Market packs: for starting seeds of fast-growing annuals and vegetables that won't be growing indoors more than a few weeks before being transplanted.

Buying a dozen or so 3½-inch pots, and the same number of 4-inch pots, will provide a good collection of containers to get you started. If you have a choice between square and round pots, choose the square ones; they fit together a bit more snugly, so you'll save some space, and they are less likely to tip over.

It's also smart to buy a few flats (trays) when you purchase your pots. Standard-size flats are usually about 1 foot wide and 20 inches long. Sometimes you can find half-flats, which are about 1 foot square; these are handy for smaller groups of pots. Some flats come with holes in the bottom; others don't have them. Those without holes are great for indoor use because they catch water that drains out of the pots. Those with drainage holes are a must for outdoor use; otherwise, they'll hold rainwater and flood your pots.

PICK A GROWING MEDIUM

Garden-supply stores and catalogs may offer a dizzying array of prepackaged growing media along with their selection of containers. Fortunately, you can get great results with just a few basic materials.

Because roots need both air and water for healthy growth, the key to choosing any medium is understanding its aeration (how much air it holds) and its moisture retention (how much water it holds). An ideal medium will hold the proper balance of air and water to meet the needs of your seeds or plants. To create this balance, most good growing media are a mix of at least two ingredients. Seed-starting mixes, for instance, are generally based on peat moss, which holds plenty of moisture to support the limited root systems of young seedlings. Of course, even seedling roots need some air for good growth, so the peat is usually mixed with a coarse material, such as perlite, to keep the peat moss loose and prevent waterlogging. Most garden centers stock at least one kind of commercial seed-starting mix; buy a bag of one kind to start with. As you gain experience, you may want to experiment with other brands, or fine-tune your favorite mix by adding more peat or perlite.

If you plan to propagate plants by cuttings (sections of stems, roots, or leaves), you'll also want to purchase one bag of perlite and one of vermiculite. Peat-based mixes tend to hold too much water for cuttings, so you'll want to create a looser growing medium. Mixing equal parts of perlite and vermiculite will provide a good balance of aeration and moisture retention for most cuttings.

Finding a Happy Medium

Whether you buy a prepackaged growing medium or mix your own, it's helpful to know what ingredients are available, along with their benefits and drawbacks. Here's an overview of the materials you're most likely to find, either as part of a commercial mix or sold separately.

Peat Moss: A key part of both seed-starting mixes and growing mixes, peat moss holds ample amounts of water. While it doesn't contribute much in the way of nutrients, it does hold a good supply of the nutrients you add when you fertilize. Peat moss tends to be somewhat acidic, so commercial mixes often include a bit of ground limestone to raise the pH level to near neutral.

Perlite: This lightweight material is actually volcanic rock that has been exposed to high heat and "popped" like popcorn. The result is irregularly shaped white granules that crumble into a powder when you crush them. Perlite is so loose that water (and the nutrients dissolved in the water) drains through it quickly. In fact, coarse perlite used alone may dry out too quickly for good root growth. For this reason, it is usually mixed with some other ingredient — generally peat for

seed-starting or growing mixes and vermiculite for cutting mixes.

Soil: Regular garden soil is a poor choice for starting seeds or rooting cuttings in containers. With regular watering, most soils will quickly pack down, squeezing out needed air and suffocating your plants' roots. Also, soil straight from your garden may contain weed seeds, pests, and diseases that can harm tender seedlings and cuttings. Some commercial potting mixes do include some soil to add weight and nutrients as well as increase the water retention, and these work well for growing larger seedlings and already-rooted cuttings.

Vermiculite: This popular propagation material is created by exposing mica to high heat. This process expands the thin layers, creating small, golden brown, somewhat shiny flakes that tend to smear when you crush them. Vermiculite holds a useful amount of moisture while allowing excess water to drain away. This versatile material can be used alone for starting seeds or cuttings, but it also works well combined with perlite for cuttings or peat for seed-starting or growing larger plants.

Once your seedlings are established or your cuttings have rooted, you'll need one other kind of growing medium to support these larger plants. Growing mixes are blended to hold more air than seed-starting mixes and more water than cutting mixes. Most of these include peat moss and perlite and/or vermiculite, along with added nutrients. A variety of commercial growing mixes is available. Those labeled "potting soil" may include some real soil or compost; soilless mixes contain no soil. As with your seed-starting mix, choose one and use it for a while. As you gain experience, you can switch to another brand, add more of certain ingredients to improve aeration or moisture retention, or blend your own growing mix from scratch.

Make Your Own Mix

Commercially blended mixes are convenient for a variety of home propagation projects. They are easy to handle, fairly inexpensive, and relatively "clean" (free of contamination by disease organisms). But if you'd rather make your own, here are a few basic recipes to get you started. As you gain experience, try adjusting the proportions and ingredients to tailor the mix to the needs of your particular plants.

Seed-Starting Mix
2 parts peat moss
1 part perlite or vermiculite

Cutting Mixes
1 part perlite
1 part vermiculite
Or:
1 part peat moss
1 part perlite or vermiculite

Growing Mix
2 parts peat moss
1 part perlite
1 part vermiculite

NOTE: To support plants growing in this mix, fertilize regularly with liquid fertilizer or incorporate a balanced commercial fertilizer into the mix before planting, at the rate recommended on the package for container plants. Commercial growing mixes also usually include lime — approximately 5 level tablespoons of finely ground dolomitic limestone per bushel of finished mix — to counteract the acidity of the peat moss.

SELECT A SITE

As most of us don't have the luxury of a home greenhouse, we have to make do with slightly less than ideal growing conditions, at least for indoor propagation projects. (For pointers on outdoor propagation structures, see "Cold Frames" on page 11 and "Creating and Using Nursery Beds" on page 18.) The three things to consider when choosing a spot for indoor propagation are the light, temperature, and ventilation.

Light

For healthy growth, your young plants will need at least 12 hours of light a day. In most homes, it can be a challenge to provide this much natural light. If you are just starting a few pots of seeds or cuttings, you can manage with just a few sunny windowsills. Save south-facing windows for your seedlings, since they need as much light as they can get. The bright but less direct sun in an east or west-facing window is generally better for cuttings.

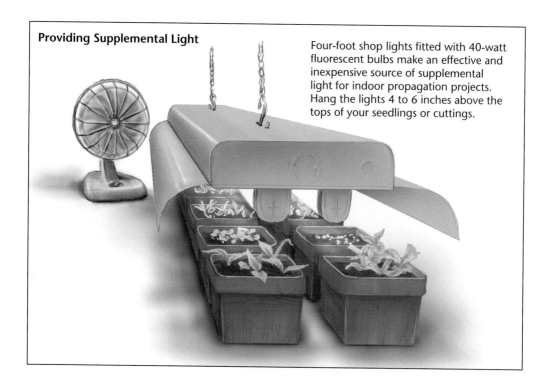

Providing Supplemental Light

Four-foot shop lights fitted with 40-watt fluorescent bulbs make an effective and inexpensive source of supplemental light for indoor propagation projects. Hang the lights 4 to 6 inches above the tops of your seedlings or cuttings.

Where window space is limited, you'll need to provide supplemental light for your new plants until conditions are right to move them outside. Many garden-supply catalogs offer commercially produced seed-starting setups, with multiple shelves and special plant growth lights. These are great if you have the space and the money. But here's one place where you can save plenty of money by creating your own light setups. Every home center sells 4-foot "shop lights" — fixtures that hold two long narrow fluorescent bulbs — usually for less than $15. Just one shop light can provide ample light for two full flats of cuttings or seedlings. If you need more illumination, buy more than one light, and set them up 6 to 12 inches apart. Hang the lights from the ceiling, or build simple supports out of wood or PVC pipe, and hang the lights from them. Suspend the lights from chains or cords so that you can adjust their height as your plants grow. Keep the lights 4 to 6 inches above the tops of your plants.

If the lights you purchase don't already have bulbs, purchase regular 4-foot, 40-watt fluorescent bulbs. They usually cost around $1 each, as opposed to the special plant growth lights, which can cost four to six times as much. The less expensive bulbs will provide good results and save you quite a bit of money. Plan on replacing the bulbs at least every other year; once a year is better.

It's definitely worth investing in a timer (generally less than $20) to turn your lights on and off automatically. Leave the lights on 14 to 16 hours a day.

Temperature

Indoors, temperatures around 70°F are ideal for most seedlings and cuttings. Some plants prefer a fairly constant temperature, although a drop of 5° to 10°F at night usually won't reduce your chance of success. If you don't keep your house this warm, don't despair; it's really the growing medium that needs to be warm, not the air around the plants. In fact, a combination of warm soil and somewhat cooler air will often give excellent results, with vigorous root growth and compact, sturdy top growth. You can create these conditions by setting your seed and cutting pots on top of your refrigerator, or on a board atop a radiator, but it can be tricky to get adequate light in these spots. If you plan to grow more than a few pots of seeds or cuttings, it's worth investing in a propagation (heating) mat, which you can use under your shop lights. Prices range widely, from around $30 for a windowsill-width mat to around $150 for a professional-quality mat with

an adjustable thermostat. For about $50, you can get a mat the size of a nursery flat which should serve the purpose for most of your propagation projects.

Ventilation

For healthy growth, plants need a balance of humidity and air circulation. Warm, stagnant air can encourage the development of disease and pest problems, while cold drafts can injure tender growth. Fortunately, it's fairly easy to control ventilation conditions. Covering pots with molded plastic "humidity domes" or clear plastic bags can help maintain the needed moisture around new seedlings and cuttings. As the young plants grow, remove the covers to allow for better air circulation. If diseases are still a problem, you can improve air movement by setting a small table fan (roughly 6 inches across or less), turned on low, a few feet away from your young plants. The fan doesn't need to blow directly on the plants; just have it stir the air around their tops.

CHOOSE TOOLS AND EQUIPMENT

A few other miscellaneous tools will prove useful for your propagation projects. A sharp pair of pruning shears is invaluable for many tasks, including taking cuttings, trimming back top growth on divisions, and snipping rooted layers from the parent plant. A sharp knife is also handy for a variety of jobs, from trimming cuttings and separating divisions to nicking the bark on woody stems to promote rooting during layering. In fact, it's handy to keep two knives: a small, very sharp one for cuttings and a larger one for other tasks.

You'll also find plenty of uses for a garden trowel, as well as a spade and/or spading fork, for digging up established plants for propagation or setting out new plants.

As you shop for your pots, growing medium, and other materials, you'll probably see other specialized tools and supplies available as well. While most of these have their purposes, there's no need to buy them when you're getting started. As you gain more experience, you may find certain items helpful, such as hormone powders or dips for encouraging root development on cuttings. Waiting to buy these specialty items until you really need them will prevent you from wasting money on a lot of useless gadgets and supplies.

Cold Frames

If you live in a cold-winter area and are short of indoor space for seedlings, consider building a cold frame. Nestled in the frame, your seedlings will receive ample sunlight but be protected from cold and wind.

A cold frame is simply a bottomless box with a movable top. The top is sloped so that water and melting snow will run off. Commercially made frames are available, but it's easy to make one yourself. For the top, salvage some old storm windows or a piece of Plexiglas; then size the rest of the frame to suit the material you've found for the top. To ensure a sloped top, use a length of 1×8 lumber for the front and an equal length of 1×12 for the back. To make the sides, cut two more equal pieces of 1×12. Then cut the top of each side on a slant, with the resulting width running from 12 inches at the back to 8 inches at the front. Screw or nail the sides together. Paint or stain the wooden parts, if desired. Rest the frame on the ground, and bank soil around the bottom to seal the gaps. Set the cover on top — attach it with hinges or just leave it loose.

Sunlight provides the only heat for your frame, so you'll need to pay close attention to the temperature inside. During the winter, bank hay or straw bales, compost, or leaves against the outside of the frame for insulation. For extra protection on cold nights, cover the top with an old quilt or blanket.

Overheating is a more common and serious problem. A little sunlight can quickly heat the air in a frame to plant-killing temperatures. If you are home during the day and can monitor your cold frame, use sticks to prop open a hinged top for ventilation, or slide off a loose top partially or completely. If you can't be home to maintain the frame, check your local garden center or mail-order supplier; many sell a hydraulic gadget filled with temperature-sensitive fluids that will automatically open and close the top.

Besides sheltering seedlings, cold frames are a big help for other propagation projects. You can use them to shelter newly potted cuttings and divisions or to protect young perennials, shrubs, vines, and trees during the winter. For a little construction effort, you'll enjoy the benefits year-round.

START WITH HEALTHY PLANTS AND SEEDS

To get healthy, vigorous new plants, you need to start with healthy parent plants and seeds. Plants that are stressed by pest or disease problems are less likely to recover well from propagation, and even if they do, you'll end up with six or a dozen problem plants, instead of just one. Knowing what to look for before choosing plants or seeds can help ensure the best possible results from your propagation projects.

Check Plants for Pests

Before dividing, layering, or taking cuttings from a plant, look carefully for signs of pests, especially the smaller ones, such as aphids, spider mites, thrips, and whiteflies. Infestations of any of these pests can seriously weaken a plant. Many insects can also spread diseases as they feed, doing double damage.

Aphids. Aphids are small insects, about half the size of a grain of rice, and they come in many colors, including green, yellow, red, black, and gray. They tend to cluster on shoot tips, stems, buds, and the undersides of leaves. They suck the plant sap, causing yellowing and distorted growth.

Mites. Also called spider mites, these minute, usually reddish pests feed on the undersides of plant leaves. While the pests themselves are difficult to see with the unaided eye, you may see tiny webs on the undersides of the leaves or completely covering the leaves. You may also spot the damage: yellow speckled areas that turn into bronzed or pale patches on leaves and growing tips.

Thrips. Thrips are also tiny, with slender bodies and narrow, fringed wings. These fast-moving pests feed on leaves, stems, buds, flowers, and fruits. While you probably won't be able to see the pests themselves, you'll see the damage they cause: yellowish or silvery speckling or streaking.

Whiteflies. Roughly the same size as aphids, whiteflies are small white insects that congregate and feed on the undersides of leaves. When you brush the plant, the adults fly up in a little cloud. (They somewhat resemble dandruff, hence the common name "flying dandruff.") Their feeding weakens the plant and can produce some yellowing.

Selecting Healthy Plants

Always choose healthy, pest-free plants to propagate from. If you find any signs of pests such as aphids, mites, thrips, or whiteflies, spray with insecticidal soap to control the problem before gathering cuttings.

Mites: Tiny ($1/150$- to $1/50$-inch-long) red-brown spiderlike pests that cause yellow- to bronze-stippled leaves with webbing on leaves and shoot tips.

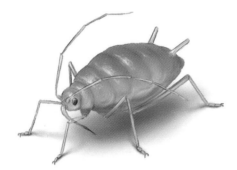

Aphids: Pale green to pinkish or red $1/10$-inch-long insects that cause yellowing and distorted growth on leaves or shoots.

Thrips: Tiny ($1/50$-inch-long) orange-brown insects that cause grayish silver stripes along tops of leaves.

Whiteflies: Small ($1/20$-inch-long) white mothlike insects on undersides of leaves with some yellowing of leaves.

If you spot signs of these or any other pests, you'll need to control the problem before you propagate from the affected plant. Insecticidal soap spray, available in garden centers and from garden-supply catalogs, will control the pests just mentioned and many others when used according to the label directions.

Inspect Plants for Diseases

Plant diseases can attack many parts of a plant and cause a wide variety of symptoms. Sometimes, the symptoms are very obvious, such as the dusty gray patches of powdery mildew, the orange spots of rust, or the tumorlike growths of crown gall. Other times, you may just notice that a plant's growth is not as vigorous as it should be. Diseases are generally difficult to control, so avoid propagating from any plant you suspect is diseased, at least until you can determine the cause and find out what options you have to deal with that particular problem. (For help, refer to an illustrated book on common plant problems, such as *Taylor's Weekend Gardening Guide: Organic Pest & Disease Control.*)

Evaluate Overall Plant Vigor

Propagating from a strong parent plant will help ensure success with division, cuttings, and layering. While the best condition for the parent plant will vary depending on the season and the technique you're using, ideally, the plant should be vigorous enough to be producing moderate new growth each year. If the plant isn't making much new growth, it may be slow to root from cuttings or recover from division. Excessively lush, lanky growth isn't desirable either, so don't be tempted to fertilize heavily to promote growth. Regular feeding with a general garden fertilizer according to package directions should encourage the right level of new growth.

Scrutinize Seeds for Problems

Good-quality seed is relatively uniform in size and color. Commercially packed seeds are generally a safe bet, as seed companies have to follow strict guidelines on seed quality. If you get seeds from friends or seed exchanges, however, it's worth taking a few minutes to inspect them before sowing. You should not see any seeds that are noticeably different mixed in; these may be weed seeds. You should also not see any pests or signs of pest damage, such as holes in the seeds.

CHOOSING THE RIGHT TECHNIQUE

For most plants, there is no one right way to propagate them; it's a matter of experimenting with different techniques to see which works best for your plants and conditions. Happily, most plants respond well to several techniques, so your chances of success are quite good. The key is to match the technique with the plant you are working with and the season you are working in. "Propagating Techniques Season by Season" will help you choose the best method for your situation. Once you've selected a technique, turn to that chapter — "Growing from Seed" on page 21, "Multiplying by Dividing" on page 51, "Taking Cuttings" on page 73, or "Layering Established Plants" on page 105 — to find complete details.

HANDLING YOUNG PLANTS

Once you've gathered materials and started your propagation projects, you're well on your way to filling your garden with plenty of new plants. But before those new plants are ready for the garden, you'll need to give them a little special care to help them make the transition. Moving from the sheltered conditions of the propagation pot or bed to the more variable conditions of the open garden is stressful for young plants. Hardening them off is one way to help them make the move. Another option is to settle them in the temporary quarters of a nursery bed.

Hardening Off

When you grow seedlings or cuttings indoors, you give them the best possible growing conditions: adequate light, moderate temperatures, careful watering, and moderate air circulation. But plants growing outdoors don't have those luxuries; they have to cope with intense sunlight, fluctuating temperatures, and drying winds. Fortunately, plants are remarkably adaptable, so they can adjust to these difficult conditions if you give them a little help. The process of gradually exposing indoor-grown plants to outdoor conditions is called hardening off.

About two weeks before you are ready to move your plants outside, stop fertilizing, and cut back on watering. After a week of this, set the plants outdoors in a sheltered spot — perhaps a shady corner of a porch, or under a bushy shrub.

Propagating Techniques Season by Season

Season	Annuals	Perennials	Bulbs	Shrubs & Vines	Trees
Early to midspring	Sow seed for summer bloom. Take and root cuttings of overwintered plants.	Sow seed indoors or outdoors. Divide summer- or fall-blooming plants.	Divide overwintered dahlia tubers before planting outdoors.	Divide suckering shrubs and clump-forming vines. Layer plants.	Layer plants.
Mid- to late spring	Sow seed for summer-to-fall bloom.	Sow seed outdoors.			
Early to midsummer	Sow seed for fall bloom.	Sow seed outdoors.	Sow seed outdoors.		
Mid- to late summer	Take stem cuttings to root and overwinter indoors.	Take stem cuttings to root indoors or outdoors. Sow seed outdoors.	Divide spring bloomers. Sow seed outdoors.	Take stem cuttings and root indoors or outdoors.	Take stem cuttings and root indoors or outdoors.
Early to midfall		Sow seed outdoors. Divide spring- or summer-blooming plants.	Divide summer bloomers. Sow seed outdoors.		Sow seed outdoors.
Mid- to late fall		Root cuttings.	Sow seed outdoors.	Take stem cuttings and root outdoors. Divide suckering shrubs and clump-forming vines.	Take stem cuttings and root outdoors. Sow seed outdoors.
Late fall to late winter	Sow seed for spring and summer bloom.	Sow seed outdoors in late fall, indoors in late winter.	Sow seed outdoors.	Sow seed outdoors in late fall, indoors in late winter.	Sow seed outdoors in late fall, indoors in late winter.

A sheltered site is ideal for hardening off new plants. Hedges and a fence protect these seedlings from wind, and trees shade the hottest rays of the sun.

Leave them outside for an hour or two during the day, then bring them inside. Over the next few days, leave them out for a few more hours each day, in increasingly brighter spots, until they are used to being outside for a full day. If you are usually away from home on weekdays, start by setting plants out on a Saturday for two hours, Sunday for half a day, and all day Monday in a shady spot; then set them in sunnier sites each day.

A cold frame can provide ideal shelter for hardening off young plants, especially if it is equipped with a device that will automatically raise and lower the lid. You'll also want to lay a screen over the top for the first few days so that your plants aren't exposed to strong sun right away. For details on making and maintaining these handy structures, see "Cold Frames" on page 11.

Keep in mind that your young plants growing outdoors will dry out more quickly than they did in the house, so be sure to check their growing mix daily, and water if needed.

Creating and Using Nursery Beds

In many cases, your young plants will be ready to move outside well before they are big enough to transplant into your beds and borders. It's handy to have a holding area or cold frame where you can group all the pots for easier daily maintenance. You'll still need to water and fertilize these plants regularly and transplant them to bigger pots as they outgrow their containers. There is a way to greatly reduce this maintenance, though: create a nursery bed.

Using a Nursery Bed

Once you create and use a nursery bed, you'll wonder how you ever got by without one. It's a perfect spot to grow small seedlings, rooted cuttings, and small divisions and layers until they are large enough for the garden. It's also a great spot to "heel in" potted perennials and shrubs until you know where you want to plant them permanently.

A nursery bed is simply an area where you can plant young plants in the ground and allow them to grow to garden size. Choose a sheltered but sunny spot, where the soil is well drained. Since this is a working area, choose an out-of-the-way site, where it won't be highly visible, or appropriate a corner of your vegetable garden. The bed can be any length you wish, but don't make it wider than 5 feet if you can reach in from both sides, or 30 inches if you can access the bed only from one side. An area of roughly 20 square feet is a good starting point. Later on, you can expand that bed or create another one, if needed.

It's worth a bit of effort to prepare the soil in your nursery bed carefully to provide the best possible growing conditions. Dig deeply to loosen the top 10 to 12 inches of soil, and dig or till in a 2- to 3-inch layer of compost to loosen and enrich the soil. If your soil is rocky or hard to dig, frame the area with timbers, rocks, or cinder blocks to create a raised bed, and fill the frame with a mix of good topsoil and compost.

You can propagate directly in your nursery bed by sowing seed or planting hardwood cuttings there, but you'll also want to leave room for setting out the smaller plants you've propagated in pots, or for rooted "layers" that aren't yet big enough for the garden. Set out the plants just as if you were planting them in the regular garden, spaced at least 8 inches apart. During the growing season, give your nursery plants good general care, paying special attention to watering during dry spells, as these youngsters are more prone than established garden plants to drying out. In spring or fall, dig up the plants that are large enough for your needs, and move them to their permanent spot in the garden. Avoid leaving plants in a nursery bed for more than two years, or their roots will spread far and wide, making them difficult to transplant.

CHAPTER 2
GROWING FROM SEED

Growing new plants from seed is one of the most fun and rewarding ways to propagate many garden plants. From just one packet of seed you can grow dozens or even hundreds of seedlings — all for the price of two or three packs of annual transplants. Of course, you aren't limited to growing just annuals or vegetables; quite a few perennials and herbs are easy to start from seed, and some will even bloom their first summer if you start them indoors in late winter. If you enjoy longer-term projects, you can grow shrubs, vines, and even trees from seed.

One thing you must remember is that starting with seed can give you somewhat unpredictable results with some plants — this can be a plus or a minus, depending on how you look at it. When you propagate a plant using a vegetative technique such as cuttings, division, or layering, you are making an exact duplicate, or clone, of a plant. As a result, in nearly all cases the new plants will look exactly like the parent — same height, same flower color, and same growth habit. With seeds, however, each new plant can look somewhat different. The difference may be so slight that you don't really notice, as with many annuals and vegetables. But in other cases, the resulting seedlings can vary considerably from the parent plant. If you enjoy variety, then this isn't a problem. But it can be disappointing if you want to propagate a particular flower color or leaf pattern.

These germinating sunflowers show the cotyledons, or seed leaves, which emerge from the seeds as they sprout. The true leaves, which follow the cotlyedons, will resemble those of the mature plant.

So how do you know if seed will give the results you hope for? Seed packets and catalogs with color photographs and/or good descriptions are excellent guides to help you guess what you'll get from the seedlings. You may also get a clue from the plant's name. If the plant has just a botanical name, such as *Iris sibirica* or *Buddleia davidii,* there's a good chance that its seedlings will look fairly similar. But if it's a perennial, shrub, vine, or tree and it has a special cultivar name, such

Perennial Cultivars from Seed

Achillea millefolium 'Summer Pastels'. 'Summer Pastels' yarrow.

Alcea rosea 'Nigra'. Black hollyhock.

Aquilegia 'Woodside Variegated'. Variegated columbine.

Asclepias incarnata 'Ice Ballet'. 'Ice Ballet' milkweed.

Campanula lactiflora 'Amethyst'. 'Amethyst' bellflower.

Delphinium grandiflorum 'Dwarf Blue Butterfly'. 'Dwarf Blue Butterfly' delphinium.

Dianthus deltoides 'Brilliancy'. 'Brilliancy' pink.

Digitalis purpurea 'Foxy'. 'Foxy' foxglove.

Echinacea purpurea 'Magnus'. 'Magnus' purple coneflower.

Erigeron speciosus 'Pink Jewel'. 'Pink Jewel' fleabane daisy.

Gaillardia × *grandiflora* 'Goblin'. 'Goblin' blanket flower.

Geranium sanguineum 'Vision'. 'Vision' hardy geranium.

Heuchera micrantha 'Palace Purple'. 'Palace Purple' heuchera.

Lavandula angustifolia 'Lady'. 'Lady' English lavender.

Liatris spicata 'Kobold'. 'Kobold' blazing star.

Lobelia 'Fan Hybrids'. 'Fan Hybrids' lobelias.

Lychnis coronaria 'Angel Blush'. 'Angel Blush' rose campion.

Monarda didyma 'Panorama Mix'. 'Panorama Mix' bee balm.

Penstemon digitalis 'Husker Red'. 'Husker Red' penstemon.

Platycodon grandiflorus 'Sentimental Blue'. 'Sentimental Blue' balloon flower.

Rudbeckia hirta 'Indian Summer'. 'Indian Summer' black-eyed Susan.

Verbascum 'Southern Charm'. 'Southern Charm' mullein.

Veronica spicata 'Blue Bouquet'. 'Blue Bouquet' veronica.

Viola sororia 'Freckles'. 'Freckles' violet.

as *Iris sibirica* 'Super Ego' or *Buddleia davidii* 'Dark Knight', don't count on the seedlings having the same height, habit, and color as the parent plant. In this case, you're better off propagating vegetatively by cuttings, division, or layering. There are some exceptions to this rule of thumb: see "Perennial Cultivars from Seed" on page 22 for a list of perennials that do come true from seed.

Keep in mind that the variability of seedlings can also bring welcome surprises. If you have a lot of space to fill, a bit of variability can add interest to mass plantings of seed-grown plants. Or you may find a seedling with a particularly beautiful flower color or form; then you can propagate it vegetatively to maintain that special trait.

A cultivar (from cultivated variety) is a special population of plants that exhibit certain desirable traits. By definition, cultivars are maintained by human intervention — they're cultivated in gardens and prized because of special traits such as a unique flower color, special flower form, compact growth habit, or disease resistance. Each particular selection is given a special name — you can recognize them because they're set off from the botanical or common name by single quotes: *Phlox carolina* 'Miss Lingard' phlox or 'Foxy' foxglove, for example.

Sometimes cultivars come from natural variants that people have spotted growing in a garden, such as a cream-colored marigold growing in a bed of yellow ones. Other times, breeders have deliberately cross-pollinated two plants to get offspring that have a certain combination of both parents' traits.

Quite often, cultivars of perennials are reproduced vegetatively or asexually, meaning by cuttings, division, or layering. This ensures that the offspring will be exact copies, or clones, of the desirable selection. But there are also sexually reproduced cultivars, which you can grow from seed. In these cases, called strains, the offspring have minimal variability, so a crop of seedlings will look relatively uniform.

Seed-grown cultivars can be a real boon if you need many new plants for your garden. For the price of a seed packet, you can produce dozens of new plants at a fraction of the cost of buying asexually propagated cultivars. Here's a rundown of just some of the perennial cultivars that you can grow from seed; new ones appear in seed catalogs each year. With any seed-grown cultivar, it's important to rogue out (remove) any seedlings that don't resemble the others so that the remaining seedlings will closely resemble each other.

But before you start thinking about finding exciting new plants, you first need to start the seeds. The secret to success with any seed is providing the ideal germination conditions. Some seeds just need warmth and moisture; others need to be cold and moist. Some require light to germinate, others must be in the dark. Fortunately, you'll rarely have to guess what conditions your seeds prefer, because generations of gardeners have already done the experimenting for you. In this chapter, you'll learn all about the seed-starting process, from obtaining the seeds to getting them established in your garden.

SEED SOURCES

One of the greatest things about starting seeds is that your options for growing new plants are virtually unlimited. You can order from a single mail-order seed company year after year and always find something new to try. Or you can get on the mailing lists of smaller companies that specialize in certain areas, such as fragrant plants, herbs, or unusual vegetables. For even more exotic seeds, you can join plant societies with seed exchanges, where seeds are donated by and distributed among interested members. (See "Shop Seed Exchanges for Uncommon Seeds" on page 25 for information on exchanges and a list of organizations that have them.) If you have access to the Internet, you can even buy seeds from or swap with gardeners all over the world!

Buying Seed

Most gardeners start with commercially packaged seeds, sold through mail-order catalogs or in displays at their local garden center. Prices can vary widely, depending on how new or unusual the plant is and how many seeds are in the packet. If you are looking for the newest color of impatiens or petunias, you may find only one or two sources, and you'll have to pay what they're asking. But when you are shopping for more common seeds, it's worth comparing prices. Some smaller companies specialize in selling smaller packages of seed for very reasonable prices. Besides paying less money, you'll also have less leftover seed to deal with.

Mail-order catalogs are a great resource for seed-starting gardeners. Catalogs plastered with glossy color photos aren't necessarily better than less colorful counterparts; in fact, their products are often more expensive. But if you are just start-

Shop Seed Exchanges for Uncommon Seeds

Seed exchanges sponsored by plant societies and organized by member volunteers can be excellent sources of unusual seeds. Each year, members collect and contribute seed from their own gardens, then volunteers package them and make them available to all members of the society, usually for a small fee. (Donors usually get first choice and/or extra seeds for their trouble.) The list of seeds available generally reflects the specialized nature of the society. Some may offer mainly hardy perennials, rock garden plants, or heirloom vegetables; others list a wide variety of annuals, perennials, trees, shrubs, and vines.

There are a few things you should be aware of before ordering seeds through a seed exchange. Seed from exchanges can be quite variable in quality. Unlike commercial seed, which is collected, packaged, and stored by professionals, volunteers provide the work force for seed exchanges. The seed may have been gathered before it was completely mature, it may include a lot of debris with the good seed, or it may not have been dried properly before storage. It's also not uncommon to find that the seed you grew as one thing turns out to be something different. Lists also vary widely in the information they provide about the seeds. In some cases, all you'll get is the plant's name; you'll have to do the research to find out the germination and growing requirements.

Still, seed exchanges are great fun. Each year they are eagerly supported and anticipated by devotees. For many avid seed-starters,

exchanges are their only source for really rare and unusual seeds.

If you'd like to get involved in a group with a seed exchange, write to any of the organizations below for membership information. Also check out Barbara Barton's *Gardening by Mail*, 5th edition (Houghton Mifflin, 1997). Besides listing over 1,000 mail-order nurseries and seed companies, it also includes contact information for many other horticultural societies you can join.

Flower and Herb Exchange
3076 North Winn Road
Decorah, IA 52101

Hardy Plant Society/Great Britain
c/o Mrs. Pam Adams
Little Orchard
Great Comberton, Nr. Pershore
Worcestershire WR10 3DP
Great Britain

Hardy Plant Society/Mid-Atlantic Group
c/o Sylvia Coopman
20 Crown Oak Drive
Chester Springs, PA 19425

North American Rock Garden Society
c/o Executive Secretary
P.O. Box 67
Millwood, NY 10546

Seed Savers Exchange
3076 North Winn Road
Decorah, IA 52101

ing out, photographs can be very helpful, as they'll show you what to expect from your seedlings. Catalogs with good descriptions are also handy, as they may tell you things about each plant that you can't tell by looking at a picture — whether a plant is disease-resistant or heat-tolerant, for example. Here again, comparison shopping makes sense. If you see a plant that you like in a photo-packed catalog, check to see if another company sells the same seeds at a lower price. Shipping costs for seed orders are usually minimal, and the savings can be worth it.

Seed catalogs start arriving in early winter, usually in late November and December. As they arrive, gather them in a box or a pile on your desk, then sit down after the holidays to look through them and make out your orders. It may seem strange to think about buying seeds when the weather outside is anything but balmy, but flipping through seed catalogs is a great way to beat the winter blues, and getting your orders in early means you'll get faster service. The longer you wait to order, the longer you'll wait for your seeds, and you may not get them by the ideal planting time. (While you won't be planting many annual flowers and vegetables until spring, some perennials need extra time, so you may want to sow their seeds in late January or early February.)

When you shop through catalogs — especially glossy, colorful ones — it can be hard to control the urge to buy packets of all those exciting, gorgeous plants. But remember that not all those plants are equally easy to grow. While garden centers tend to stock only the easiest, most dependable seeds, catalogs cater to customers of all experience levels. When you are just starting out, look for descriptions or symbols that indicate that a plant is easy to raise from seed.

Collecting Seed

You don't always have to buy seed; you can also collect it yourself, from your own garden or those of your friends (with their permission, of course). It's a great way to save money, especially if you need large quantities of seed. It also makes sense if you need just a few seeds. Saving seed is also a practical way to keep many of your favorite annuals from year to year.

To avoid disappointment, you do need to keep in mind that the seeds you collect may not produce seedlings that resemble the plant you gathered them from. This is true of all seeds, but it's especially important to remember when deciding which ones to collect. The annual and vegetable seeds you buy from a commercial seed company are often hybrids — the result of controlled crosses between carefully chosen parent plants. (To produce the crops of hybrid seed they sell, breeders repeat these crosses annually.) Plants grown from these careful crosses exhibit certain desirable traits, such as compact growth or a special flower color. If you collect seeds from the hybrid plants that result, however, don't expect the resulting seedlings to show the same special traits. Some may, but most will look more like one of the original parent plants.

So how do you know which plants are hybrids? Sometimes you'll just have to experiment: collect the seeds and see what you get. But often you can tell from the plant's name, or its seed packet or catalog description: look for the word "hybrid" or the symbol "F_1."

When you know which plants you want to collect from, plan to check them every few days after they begin to bloom. As plants flower and set seed at different times of the year, there are no hard and fast rules about when to collect each one. Some ripen and drop their seeds all at once; others hold their seeds for months. In general, seeds are ready to collect when they are firm, full, and dark. If they are enclosed in a pulpy fruit, they are usually ripe enough to gather about a week before the fruit turns soft and juicy. Sometimes it can be tricky to catch the seeds before they fall or are eaten by animals. The trick here is to enclose the developing seed head or pod in a paper or cloth bag, or the toe cut from a pair of old nylon stockings. (Don't use a plastic bag — the seeds may rot.) The covering will catch and protect the seeds, so you can gather them at your convenience.

Most of the time, you can remove ripe seeds from a plant with a bare or gloved hand. You may want to remove only the fruiting body or seed head, or it may be easier to clip the stems and separate the seeds later. Place seeds or fruits in paper or cloth sacks; green leaves, stems, and fleshy parts of fruits can quickly rot — and possibly destroy the seeds — if you enclose them in plastic bags or glass jars. Put your collected seeds in a warm, sheltered location for further drying. You can leave small quantities of seeds in their bags and stir them occasionally, but it's best to spread the seeds over sheets of newspaper for quick and thorough drying.

Separating dried seeds from leaves, stems, and other plant debris requires experience and ingenuity. You can separate seeds from chaff by using a stack of homemade or commercial screens, each of a different mesh size, with the largest

mesh on top and the smallest on the bottom. Place the seeds and debris on the top screen, and shake the stack. The screens will filter out particles of different sizes, and with any luck, one screen will contain pure seed. To separate heavy seed from lighter chaff, carefully drop small portions in front of a small fan. With some practice, you'll find the ideal distance from the fan so that only the seeds fall and the trash blows away.

Seeds in fleshy fruits, such as roses and tomatoes, need cleaning immediately after collection to avoid molding and rotting. Methods include crushing the fruit with a rolling pin, forcing the fruit through screens, or crushing the fruit by hand in water. Put the crushed fruit in a bucket of water, and skim the debris and pulp off the top. Drain the water, spread the seeds on a screen for drying and storage, or plant them immediately.

After a week or so in a warm, dry spot, your seeds will be ready for storage. Place clean, dry seeds in paper envelopes (coin envelopes are great for this), labeled with the name of the plant and the collection date. If needed, tape the corners of the envelopes so that small seeds don't escape. Placing the packets in a closed, airtight, and moisture-proof container will help to keep the seeds dry.

STORING SEED

After a year or two of starting seeds, you'll likely have quite a collection of half-used seed packets. Whether you buy seed or collect your own, the way you store it will have an effect on its quality.

Store seeds in a cool, dry place; many seed-savers keep their seeds in their refrigerator. No seed will remain viable (able to germinate) long in the hot, humid conditions found it kitchens, attics, damp cellars, or greenhouses. Seeds stored under less-than-ideal conditions may fail to germinate properly or may germinate more slowly and with less vigor than properly stored seeds.

Testing Germination

With proper storage, most seeds stay viable for several years, so you don't need to buy new packets each year. Exactly how long they maintain their viability can vary, though, so you may want to test them before counting on them to produce all the plants you need.

A simple way to test germination is by placing 10 seeds, spaced about 1 inch apart, on a moist paper towel. Carefully roll up the towel, place it in a plastic bag, and close the bag loosely. Label the bag and set it in a warm place. Check the seed packet to see how long you can expect the seed to take to germinate. Around that time, open the bag, unroll the towel, and count how many of the seeds have sprouted. This will tell you the germination percentage. If fewer than seven seeds (70 percent) have germinated, sow more thickly than usual. If the percentage is less than 50, you're probably best off buying new seeds.

This testing technique works best for annuals and vegetables, which tend to germinate within a few weeks when kept warm and moist. With other kinds of seeds, it's just as easy to go ahead and sow them, in pots indoors or outside, or directly into a nursery bed, and see what happens.

Testing Germination

Don't throw away seeds you have left over from previous years; there's still a chance they may germinate. You can test the viability of many seeds by placing them on a moist paper towel as shown here.

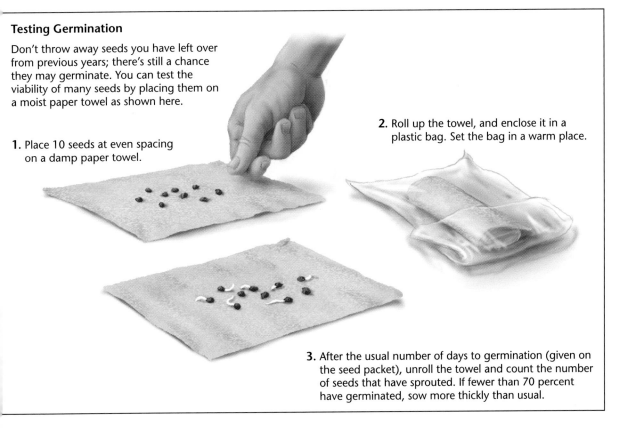

1. Place 10 seeds at even spacing on a damp paper towel.

2. Roll up the towel, and enclose it in a plastic bag. Set the bag in a warm place.

3. After the usual number of days to germination (given on the seed packet), unroll the towel and count the number of seeds that have sprouted. If fewer than 70 percent have germinated, sow more thickly than usual.

DECIDING WHEN TO SOW

You have your seeds, and you have your supplies — now you're ready to sow. Late winter to midspring is the busiest time for most seed sowers, but you can sow seeds virtually any time of year, depending on what you are growing. Your best reference for deciding sowing times is the information on the seed packet. Most companies provide detailed information to help you get the best results. But if you don't have access to this guidance, you'll have to rely on some basic knowledge to pick the appropriate sowing time.

Late-Winter and Spring Sowing

Late winter through early spring is the ideal time to start many kinds of seeds indoors, while early to late spring is generally best for sowing directly into the garden. Best bets for sowing in these seasons include most annual flowers, herbs, and vegetables. Early sowing indoors can also allow some perennials to flower their first summer in the garden. With other perennials, you'll have to wait a year or more for first bloom.

When sowing indoors, time the sowing so that the plants will be a good size when you move them outdoors. But don't start them too early either, or they could get overgrown and crowded. The benchmark most gardeners use is their last frost date. While the exact date of the last spring frost will vary from year to year, you can use the average date for your area. To find out the last frost date for your area, talk to gardening friends in your neighborhood, or ask at a local nursery or garden center. Once you know that date, mark it on your calendar, then count backward to determine your sowing dates. If the seed packet doesn't give you guidelines, figure on starting annuals and vegetables four to six weeks before your last frost date, and perennials around eight weeks before your last frost date.

Outdoor sowing is a little trickier to time without guidance from a seed packet. Some seeds grow best when sown as soon as the soil thaws and dries out enough to dig. With others, you need to wait until after the last frost date, when the soil has warmed up a bit. When you want to sow outside but don't know what your seeds need, try sowing some of them two to three weeks before your last frost date. If they germinate quickly, within a week or so, sow the rest (as needed) right away. Otherwise, wait until a week or two after your last frost date, and sow again.

Summer Sowing

Midsummer is a great time to sow seeds of many perennials. For some, this timing is necessary. Many early-blooming plants, especially spring-blooming wildflowers such as Virginia bluebells *(Mertensia virginica)*, twinleaf *(Jeffersonia diphylla)*, and bleeding-hearts *(Dicentra* spp.), produce seeds that are quick to dry out, so you need to plant them as soon as they ripen to get good germination (usually the following spring). For other perennials, summer sowing gives you sturdy young plants that can stay outside through the winter and reach blooming size the following year.

Fall Sowing

Some perennial, shrub, vine, and tree seeds germinate best when you sow them outdoors in fall, in pots, or in a nursery bed. If you've had poor results sowing these kinds of seed at other times of the year, try this treatment. Sowing outdoors in fall (and even into winter, if your seeds arrive late) provides the chilling period, or the periods of alternating warm and cold temperatures, that these seeds may need to start sprouting. You'll usually see seedlings emerge the following spring, although some seeds may take two or even three years to appear.

TRICKS FOR HANDLING DIFFICULT SEEDS

While many seeds are gratifyingly easy to germinate, some can be quite a challenge — at least until you figure out just what they need to get going. Experienced seed starters have come up with all kinds of tricks to get their more challenging seeds off to a good start. Here are a few seed-starting secrets you may find helpful.

The "Bag" Technique for Tiny Seeds

Seeds that dry out after sowing are much less likely to germinate; in fact, it may even kill them. Drying out isn't much of a problem with large- and medium-size seeds, especially those that are covered with growing mix or soil. But tiny seeds, especially those sown on the surface of the medium (such as begonias), may need to be misted with water several times a day to keep them moist. Fortunately, it's easy to reduce this maintenance: simply enclose the seeds — pot and all — in a

clear plastic bag. This technique also works well for starting perennial seeds that take several weeks or months to germinate.

Because high humidity encourages the development of diseases as well as seedlings, you should sterilize the surface of the growing medium before sowing. To do this, just before sowing pour boiling water over the medium, and allow excess water to drain. (Repeat the process once or twice more for even better results.) Then let the soil cool for a few minutes, sow your seeds, place the pot in the bag, and close the bag loosely. Bagged pots can sit under fluorescent lights for months without additional watering because the bag holds in moisture and keeps the humidity high around the seeds. Once seedlings have germinated, expose them gradually to the outside world. Open the top of the bag for an hour or two one day, and a few more hours the next. Then remove it and begin watering and fertilizing as usual. If you like, you can leave seedlings in the bag until they are an inch or two tall.

Nicking for Tough Seed Coats

Some seeds are enclosed in a particularly hard or tough seed coat that prevents water from getting in and starting the germination process. At the very least, it may take weeks or months for enough water to enter, slowing down sprouting. In this case, nicking or scratching the seed coat helps water enter and speeds up the process considerably. To do this, carefully use a utility knife or single-edged razor blade to chip a small hole in the seed covering. You can chip anywhere except right around the hilum, the small scar left where the seed was attached to its parent. If you can't see a scar, just stay away from any concave (pressed-in) areas on the seed. You can sow immediately after nicking the seed. Try this technique with lupines (*Lupinus* spp.), moonflower *(Calonyction aculeatum),* morning glories (*Ipomoea* spp.),

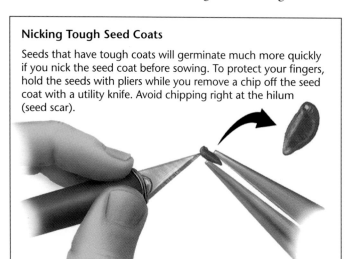

Nicking Tough Seed Coats

Seeds that have tough coats will germinate much more quickly if you nick the seed coat before sowing. To protect your fingers, hold the seeds with pliers while you remove a chip off the seed coat with a utility knife. Avoid chipping right at the hilum (seed scar).

peonies (*Paeonia* spp.), and baptisias (*Baptisia* spp.). An alternative to nicking is soaking seeds in hot (but not boiling) water for 12 to 24 hours.

Presprouting for Special Seeds

Sprouting seeds before you plant them gives you an extra measure of control — a benefit when dealing with expensive or hard-to-find seeds. Place the seeds, spaced about 1 inch apart, on one half of a full sheet of moist, strong paper towel. Fold the free half of the towel over the other, then roll or fold the towel and put it in a lightweight, clear plastic bag. Fold the bag over to close it loosely, label it with the name of the seeds and the date, and set it in a warm place.

Every week, open the bag and towel to check for germination. As seeds sprout, carefully remove them and plant them in pots of moistened seed-starting mix. Replace the remaining seeds and towel in the bag, and check again every two to three days. If none have sprouted in three months, place the bagged seeds in your refrigerator, and continue to check them weekly. Add some water if the towel begins to dry out. Transfer the seeds to a new towel if the original one gets moldy or torn. For some types of seed, you may need several three-month cycles of warmth and cold to get complete germination. But in the meantime, you'll have saved all the space and time required if you'd planted all those seeds in pots.

SOWING SEED IN CONTAINERS

To some gardeners, sowing seeds in containers may seem like a waste of time and space. But there are several distinct advantages to container sowing, so it's definitely worth considering. First, containers give you much more control of the environment around the seeds, so it's easier to provide their ideal germination conditions. You can set the pots on heat mats for extra warmth or move them outside or into a refrigerator for chilling. You'll also use clean growing medium, so there's less chance of pests, diseases, or weeds attacking or crowding out your seedlings. You can carefully monitor the moisture around container-sown seeds, so they'll be less likely to dry out. Container growing is also invaluable for getting an early start with many annuals, vegetables, and perennials. When started indoors, your container-sown seedlings can be up and growing strong weeks before outdoor-sown seedlings have even germinated.

CONTAINER-SOWING INDOORS

Once you've decided which seeds to start indoors, and you've figured out when you want to start them, you're ready to get down to the nitty gritty of seed-sowing. Start by finding a work space with plenty of room, where it doesn't matter if you spill some water or knock some seed-starting mix on the floor.

Gather Your Supplies

Collect some 2½- to 4-inch plastic pots — and/or market packs, if you are starting fast-growing annuals and vegetables — as well as a few flats to carry them

---

BEST BETS: *Sowing in Containers*

There's really no limit to the seeds you could start in containers, but some seeds benefit more than others from the special care they'll get when container-grown. Here's a rundown of some good choices for sowing indoors or outdoors in pots, and a few specific examples for each.

Seeds that need extra warmth to sprout or grow well. Start these indoors: basil, browallias (*Browallia* spp.), castor bean *(Ricinus communis)*, coleus (*Coleus* spp.), eggplant, globe amaranth (*Gomphrena* spp.), Madagascar periwinkle *(Catharanthus roseus)*, melons, peppers, tomatoes.

Tiny seeds. Start these indoors: begonias, lobelias, petunias.

Annuals that need a long growing season to bloom well. Start these indoors: cathedral bells (*Cobaea scandens)*, zonal geraniums (*Pelargonium* spp.).

Perennials that may bloom their first summer. Some perennials may bloom their first summer if seed is sown early enough indoors. These include

anise hyssops (*Agastache* spp.), black-eyed Susans (*Rudbeckia* spp.), 'Foxy' foxgloves (*Digitalis purpurea* 'Foxy'), 'Lady' lavender (*Lavandula angustifolia* 'Lady'), 'Blue Bouquet' veronica (*Veronica spicata* 'Blue Bouquet').

Expensive or hard-to-get seeds. These include the following, which germinate best in outdoor conditions: corydalis (*Corydalis* spp.), foamflowers (*Tiarella* spp.), hellebores (*Helleborus* spp.), hepaticas (*Hepatica* spp.), many bulbs, roses (*Rosa* spp.), Solomon's-seals (*Polygonatum* spp.), thalictrums (*Thalictrum* spp.), violets (*Viola* spp.).

Very small batches of seed. If you have a limited number of seeds, containers are your best bet. Start perennial, bulb, shrub, vine, and tree seeds indoors or outdoors.

Summer-sown perennials. Summer sowings of perennial seeds are best started in containers.

Annuals for container plantings. Start annuals you want for container displays indoors.

Sowing Seed Indoors

Fill a pot to within 1/4 to 1/2 inch of the rim with moist seed-starting medium. Firm the surface with the back of your fingers, then scatter seeds evenly over medium. Sprinkle a little additional medium over seed, and add a label with the name and date. Cover the finished pots with plastic and set them in a warm, bright place or under lights.

in. Some gardeners skip the pots and sow directly into the flats, but pots are generally much easier to handle. Plus, if diseases strike, they can spread quickly through a flat and wipe out hundreds of seedlings in a day or two. But if the seedlings are in pots, you've lost only one pot's worth of seedlings.

Wooden or plastic plant labels — enough to have one for each pot — and a marking pen or pencil are a must, even if you are sowing only one kind of seed on a given day. (You may think you'll remember what's in those pots, but it's remarkably easy to forget after a few weeks.) Also gather all the seeds you plan to start at this time, and a pair of scissors for opening the packets. A pair of tweezers can be useful for handling individual seeds.

You'll also need seed-starting mix, vermiculite, or whatever other medium you've chosen for starting your seeds. If you are using a mix that includes peat moss (as most commercial mixes do), it's best to moisten it before sowing, as it can be hard to wet evenly afterward. To premoisten the mix, pour it into a large bucket or tub, and add warm water (start with a quart or so of water for a bucket, or a gallon for a large tub). Knead the mix with your hands to help it absorb the

water. Keep adding more water until the mix is evenly moist. When you squeeze a handful of mix, it should stay in a ball but break apart easily if you tap it lightly. If you add too much water, just add more dry mix.

Prepare the Pots

Fill each pot to overflowing with moist mix. Use the side of your hand to level the top of the mix with the top of the pot. Using the backs of your fingers, press down the surface of the mix to firm it evenly. The final surface of the mix should be $\frac{1}{2}$ to $\frac{1}{4}$ inch below the top of the pot.

Sow the Seeds

Scatter the seeds evenly over the surface of the mix, or sow them in rows spaced about 1 inch apart. Large- and medium-size seeds are easy to handle with your fingers or tweezers, or you can just snip off one corner of the seed packet and tap them out individually.

Smaller seeds take a bit more care to sow evenly. (Remember, when you are dealing with begonias and other very small seeds, you may want to try the special technique described in "Tricks for Handling Difficult Seeds" on page 3. In this case, it's best to sterilize the surface of the mix with boiling water before sowing.) To make sowing easier, take an index card or business card, and crease it longways. Pour the seeds onto the card, and tap the card lightly with your finger to scatter them over the mix. Then use your fingers to lightly press the seeds into the surface.

The first few times you plant seeds, you may be tempted to sow thickly, "in case they don't all come up." In many cases, though, they will all come up, and you'll have a time-consuming job separating the seedlings at transplanting time. You are better off sowing them in two or more pots than trying to cram them all into one. If you decide to keep them all, they'll be much easier to transplant. Or if you have too many, you can give the extra pots to friends.

Check the seed packet for the ideal sowing depth for each kind of seed, then add that much mix to cover the seeds. Spread the mix by hand, or sift it through a screen to cover the entire surface evenly. If the packet doesn't tell you how deep to plant, use a layer of mix that's about two or three times the thickness of the seed. Don't cover very small seeds; just press them into the surface of the mix.

Care After Sowing

After sowing each pot, add a label with the name of the seed and the sowing date. If you've moistened the mix well before sowing, many seeds will germinate before they need additional water. You can help keep the seeds moist by covering the containers with sheets of clear plastic, or with molded plastic domes sold for this purpose. Don't put covered containers in direct sunlight, as temperatures inside can quickly heat up enough to kill the seeds or emerging seedlings. Instead, set them under fluorescent lights, as discussed in "Select a Site" on page 8. Remove the coverings once the seedlings emerge.

A few perennials — including columbines (*Aquilegia* spp.), hardy cyclamen (*Cyclamen* spp.), primroses (*Primula* spp.), and sea hollies (*Eryngium* spp.) — may benefit from a brief chilling period before you set them in a warm, bright place. Place each pot in a plastic bag, close the bag loosely, and set it in your refrigerator for two to three weeks. After that, move it under your fluorescent lights. You can leave the bag on until the seedlings appear.

Check the mix in uncovered containers several times a day, and never let it dry out. When you need to water, set the pots in a pan filled with an inch or so of water at room temperature or warmer; capillary action will draw the water up

A shop light with ordinary fluorescent bulbs in it will provide plenty of light for two flats of seedlings. Hang the light so that it is 4 to 6 inches above the plants. Raise the light, if necessary, as the plants grow.

through the mix. When the surface of the mix looks moist (usually within 10 to 20 minutes), remove each pot and let it drain. This system also works well for watering seedlings; just allow the top of the mix to dry slightly between soakings. Watering from below does take a little more time than top watering, but it's worth it. You won't have to worry about washing out the seeds or knocking over the seedlings, and the mix will stay evenly moist, promoting good root growth. And since the seedlings don't get wet, there's much less chance of seedling diseases getting started.

CONTAINER-SOWING OUTDOORS

If your indoor growing space is limited, or if you are starting seeds that germinate best in outdoor conditions, you can still start your seeds in pots. Of course, this works best with perennials and other seeds that can germinate in cool con-

Container-Sowing Outdoors

Outdoor sowing is a good option for perennials, shrubs, and other plants that require a period of cold temperatures before they will germinate. Fill a pot to within $1/2$ inch of the rim with moist seed-starting medium, and firm the surface. Scatter the seeds evenly over the medium, cover them with $1/8$ inch of medium followed by a $1/4$-inch layer of fine, washed gravel. Set labeled pots in a cold frame, or sink them to their rims in a nursery bed.

ditions; it's generally not practical for vegetables and herbs that need warmth to get a good start. Follow the same technique described in "Container-Sowing Indoors," earlier in this chapter, up through "Sow the Seeds." After covering the seed with the right amount of mix, top that with a 1/4- to 1/2-inch layer of fine, washed gravel; the small pebbles sold for use in aquariums usually work well. This layer keeps the mix from drying out quickly, and it also helps prevent mosses from developing and smothering your seedlings. Also add a plastic label (wooden ones can rot quickly) marked with the seed name and sowing date.

Set the pots in a cold frame, or sink them to their rims in a nursery bed or an out-of-the-way spot in the garden. It's smart to cover them with a piece of fine-mesh hardware cloth to keep mice and other animals from digging in the pots. If you like, you can surround the pots with a temporary wall of bricks and set a screen on top. Be sure to weigh down the screen with extra bricks to keep squirrels or chipmunks from crawling under it.

A nursery bed is handy for a variety of seed-sowing operations. Move slow-growing perennials started indoors or outside to a nursery bed if they need a year or two of growing time before being moved to the garden. You can also direct-sow into a nursery bed. This bed has mesh sides and a removable top to protect plants from animal pests.

TROUBLESHOOTING: *Container-Sown Seeds*

PROBLEM: Few or no seedlings appear.

Cause	Solution
Seed not mature when collected, or stored improperly.	Buy new seed and try again; store unused seed in cool, dry place.
Seeds dried out after sowing.	Water more carefully; cover seed pots with plastic to retain moisture.
Seeds rotted.	Indoors, water only when surface of mix starts to look a little dry. Mix 1 part perlite with 2 parts of seed-starting mix to improve drainage in pots.
Seeds too cold or too warm after sowing.	Check seed packet for ideal germination temperature. Set pots on a heating mat for extra warmth, or place in refrigerator for chilling.
Seeds need several seasons outdoors to sprout.	Be patient with perennials, bulbs, shrubs, vines, and trees; some may take 2 or 3 years to germinate.
Seeds dried out too much before sowing.	Sow seed of spring-flowering perennials outdoors as soon as it is ripe; don't store it.

PROBLEM: Seedlings appear, then fall over or disappear.

Cause	Solution
Damping-off (seedling diseases).	Sow again, using a bag of newly opened seed-starting mix. If reusing pots, soak them in 10 percent bleach solution (1 part bleach to 9 parts water) for 30 minutes first. Remove covers when seedlings appear. Set a fan near seedlings to improve air circulation.
Lack of water.	Prevent wilting by watering as soon as the surface of mix starts to dry out. Wilted seedlings may recover after watering but often do not perform well afterward.
Slugs or other pests.	Protect outdoor pots from slugs by sprinkling diatomaceous earth around emerging seedlings. Keep animal pests at bay with wire mesh cages.

PROBLEM: Seedlings pale and spindly.

Cause	Solution
Not enough light.	Set seedlings under fluorescent lights, hung 4 to 6 inches above tops of seedlings. Leave lights on 14 to 16 hours a day. Replace bulbs after one or two seasons.
Seedlings too warm.	Set seedlings in a cooler spot; 65° to 70°F is ideal for many seedlings.
Seedlings crowded.	Transplant to individual pots when seedlings have at least one set of "true" leaves. Sow less thickly next time.
Lack of nutrients.	Fertilize seedlings every 10 to 14 days.

Natural rainfall will take care of most of the watering, but you will need to water during dry spells. While some perennials will germinate in a few weeks, it may take months for others to appear (even years, in some cases).

TRANSPLANTING

Once your seedlings emerge, remove any covers to allow good air circulation, and give them plenty of light. Most seedlings will need transplanting only once before you move them out into the garden. When weather conditions allow you to move indoor-grown seedlings outside, gradually introduce them to outdoor conditions, as explained in "Hardening Off" on page 15.

When the first pair of true leaves have developed (after the first "seed" leaves), you can transplant indoor- or outdoor-grown seedlings into individual 2- to

Transplanting Seedlings

Seedlings are ready for transplanting as soon as the first pair of true leaves has developed. Tip out the whole potful of seedlings, lay it on its side, and tease out the seedlings one at a time with a pencil or plant label. Holding the seedling by a leaf, plant it in an individual pot of moist growing mix.

4-inch pots, or into market packs or flats (generally for fast-growing annuals only). Use a growing medium that's somewhat coarser — with more perlite and/or vermiculite — than the seed-starting mix. (For more details on selecting a growing mix, refer back to "Pick a Growing Medium" on page 5.) Moisten the growing mix before transplanting, as you did before sowing.

Several hours before transplanting, water the seedlings well. When you are ready to transplant, fill the new containers with moistened mix, to within 1/4 inch of the top. Next, carefully turn the pot of seedlings on its side, and tip the whole clump of seedlings and roots into one hand while you pull off the pot with your other hand. Lay the clump on its side on your work surface. Holding one seedling by a leaf (not the stem), use a pencil or plant label to separate its roots from the others. Now use the pencil or plant label to make a hole in the center of the new container. The hole should be just deep enough to hold the roots without bending them. Lower the seedling into the hole so that the point where the roots join the stem is even with the top of the growing mix. Use the pencil or plant label to gently push the moist mix around the roots until the mix supports the seedling when you let go of its leaf. Don't press the soil down around the seedling; just gently tap the bottom of the pot once or twice on your work surface to settle the mix around the roots. Add a little more mix, if needed, to support the seedling. Water as soon as possible after transplanting.

Watering and Fertilizing

Continue watering indoor pots from below by setting them in a pan with an inch or so of water until the surface of the mix looks moist, then letting them drain. Let the surface of the mix dry out a bit between waterings. Water outdoor pots from above as needed to keep the mix evenly moist.

Start fertilizing your seedlings when they develop their first pair of "true" leaves (the set after the first "seed" leaf or leaf pair). Start fertilizing with a liquid houseplant fertilizer, diluted to half its regular strength, or with a fertilizer specially blended for seedlings, according to the directions on the label. Feed once a week for three to four weeks. (Supply it as you would water: from below for indoor pots, from above for outdoor pots.) After that, you can use the fertilizer full strength every 10 to 14 days until they are ready for transplanting into the garden.

SOWING SEED IN THE GARDEN

Sowing seeds in pots gives you a lot of control over their environment, but some don't really need that much attention. In fact, some plants perform best when you sow their seeds right where you want them to grow, or else in a nursery bed. Outdoor-sown seeds may not germinate as quickly and uniformly as potted seeds, but they generally catch up to their indoor-sown counterparts within a few weeks (with annuals and vegetables) or months (with perennials). And in the meantime, you've saved yourself a bit of effort.

Proper timing and good soil preparation are key parts of ensuring success with direct sowing. To determine the ideal sowing time for your seeds, refer back to "Deciding When to Sow" on page 30; then plan to prepare the planting site around that time. But before you dig, make sure the soil isn't too wet or too dry; otherwise, you can destroy its loose, crumbly structure, and your seeds and plants won't sprout and grow as well later on. To check the moisture, take a handful of

BEST BETS: *Sowing Outdoors*

Outdoor sowing is a good option for many fast-growing plants, and for those that germinate best under outdoor conditions. Here are a few guidelines to help you judge which kinds of seeds are good candidates for outside sowing, either directly into the garden or in a nursery bed, and a few specific examples of each.

Many vegetables. Many popular crops can be sown directly into the garden, including beans, beets, carrots, corn, lettuce, peas, radishes, and spinach.

Plants that resent transplanting. A number of popular plants grow poorly when their roots are disturbed by transplanting and are best sown outdoors where they are to grow. These include California poppy *(Eschscholzia californica)*, dill, fennel, honesty *(Lunaria annua)*, and poppies *(Papaver* spp.).

Fast-growing annuals. Sow these in the garden where they are to grow: bachelor's buttons *(Centaurea cyanus)*, cosmos *(Cosmos bipinnatus)*, nasturtium *(Tropaeolum majus)*, sunflowers *(Helianthus* spp.).

Annuals that germinate best in cool temperatures. Sow these in the garden where they are to grow: cleome *(Cleome hasslerana)*, larkspur *(Consolida ambigua)*, love-in-a-mist *(Nigella damascena)*, pot marigolds *(Calendula officinalis)*.

Perennials with medium to large seeds. Sow these in a nursery bed for best results: daylilies *(Hemerocallis* spp.), hollyhocks *(Alcea rosea)*, irises *(Iris* spp.), peonies *(Paeonia* spp.).

Large batches of shrub, vine, and tree seeds. Sow these in a nursery bed.

soil and squeeze it. If water runs out, or if the soil stays in a tight ball when you open your hand, it is too wet. Let the soil dry out for two or three more days and test again. If the soil is too dry, it will probably just crumble apart again when you open your hand. Water the site thoroughly, then test the soil again in a day or so. When the soil stays in a clump when you open your hand but crumbles when you tap it lightly, the soil moisture is ideal for easy digging.

Prepare the site as you normally would for planting by spreading 1 to 2 inches of compost over the bed and working it into the top 8 to 10 inches of soil. Then use a garden rake to level and smooth the surface and break up soil clumps. Once the bed is prepared, do not step onto the loosened soil; otherwise, you'll compact it and undo all the work you put into fluffing it up. If you can't reach all parts of the area from the edge, lay a few broad boards over the soil, and step on those to distribute your weight while sowing. Work from the center of the bed outward, removing the boards as you are finished with them.

If you are sowing in a nursery bed instead of directly in the garden, you'll have already loosened the soil when you made the bed. (Refer back to "Creating and Using Nursery Beds" on page 18 for details.) Just use a hand fork to scratch up the surface a bit, and you are ready to plant.

Sowing in Rows

When you want a formal look for your plantings, or if you are sowing in a nursery bed, you'll probably want to plant in rows. Using a stick or the edge of a garden rake, draw shallow rows in the soil surface, about $1/2$ inch deep and 6 inches apart. Sow the seeds evenly along each row. Draw the rake lightly over the soil surface, crosswise to the rows, to cover the seeds, and firm the soil with your hand or the head of your rake. Water the area thoroughly with a fine spray. Label each row with a plastic label. Check the seedbed often (at least once a day), and water again if needed to keep the soil surface moist until seedlings appear.

Sowing in Drifts

If you want your plantings to have a more informal look, try sowing seeds in broad drifts instead of rows. This is the best approach for plants that are being sown directly in the garden where they are to grow. It helps to outline the area of each drift in the soil before planting so that you won't overlap areas when you

Sowing Seeds in Rows

Use a stick or the corner of a rake to make shallow furrows, about 1/2 inch deep and 6 inches apart. Sow seeds evenly along rows, and draw a rake over the area to cover them.

Pat the soil with your hands to firm the seedbed, add a label, and water gently to avoid washing away the seeds.

sow. Outline the pattern with a stick or the edge of your garden rake, or trace it onto the soil with a sprinkling of flour or garden lime. Scatter the seeds evenly in the desired areas, then rake lightly to scratch the seed into the soil, or sprinkle more soil on top to cover them. Firm the soil with your hand or the head of your rake. Again, it's a good idea to label the planting with a plastic marker so that you'll remember what's planted there. Water thoroughly with a fine spray after planting, and again as needed to keep the soil surface moist until seedlings appear.

Caring for Garden-Sown Seeds

Outdoor-sown seeds will need a bit of attention after they germinate. First, you'll need to thin them. It can be hard to remove some of those vigorous little

Sowing Seeds by Broadcasting

Scatter seeds evenly over raked soil, in an oblong or freeform area. Rake again, in the opposite direction, to settle the seed in the soil. Pat the soil with your hand to firm the seedbed, and add a label. Water gently, using the fine spray from a hose or a watering can with a fine rose.

seedlings, but if you don't do it when the plants are young, they will soon crowd each other as they grow. Crowded plants won't bloom as well as they would have if they had the space they needed to develop properly. Thinning in two steps, several weeks apart, takes a little more time, but it helps ensure more evenly spaced plantings. Since garden-sown seedlings are also more exposed to cold snaps and pests, thinning in two steps ensures that you'll have a healthy stand of plants if problems do occur.

Thinning

When seedlings are an inch or so tall, thin them out to stand about 2 inches apart. Snip off unwanted seedlings with scissors at ground level (pulling them out can disturb the roots of remaining seedlings), or carefully dig them up and move them to bare spots. If the seedlings are very thick, try drawing a rake lightly over the area, first one way and then the other, to thin them that way.

About three weeks later, thin your seedlings again by hand, according to the recommended spacing suggested on the seed packet. If you don't have any spac-

TROUBLESHOOTING: Garden-Sown Seeds

PROBLEM: Few or no seedlings appear.

Cause	Solution
Seed not mature when collected, or stored improperly.	Buy new seed and try again; store unused seed in cool, dry place.
Seeds dried out after sowing.	Water more carefully; cover seedbed with boards to hold in moisture; lift boards often to check seeds and remove them as soon as the first sprouts appear.
Seeds rotted.	If weather has been very damp, wait until dry weather returns and sow again. If water puddles on soil, choose a spot with better drainage for replanting, or dig deeply and work ample amounts of compost into the soil.
Seeds too cold after sowing.	Sow again in a week or two, when the weather has warmed up.

PROBLEM: Seedlings appear, then fall over or disappear.

Cause	Solution
Damping-off (seedling diseases).	Sow again when weather is warmer and drier.
Pests.	Sow again, then cover seedbed with a low wire mesh cage to keep animal pests out. Repel slugs by sprinkling diatomaceous earth around emerging seedlings.

PROBLEM: Seedlings pale and spindly.

Cause	Solution
Seedlings crowded.	Thin seedlings to 2 inches apart when they are large enough to handle, then thin again to final spacing about three weeks later.
Lack of nutrients.	Fertilize with a sprinkling of general garden fertilizer.

Thinning Seedlings

Use a blunt knife to lift clumps of small seedlings and transplant them to bare spots. Thin larger seedlings by snipping off unwanted ones at soil level.

ing guidelines to follow, try 6 to 8 inches for annuals, 4 to 6 inches for bulb seedlings, and 10 to 12 inches for other plants.

Pest and Frost Protection

If frost is predicted, cover seedbeds overnight with newspaper (one or more sheets thick) — hold the edges down with soil or pebbles. If slugs are a problem in your garden, sprinkle a ring of diatomaceous earth (available from garden centers or garden-supply catalogs) around each seedling to keep these pests at bay. Animals

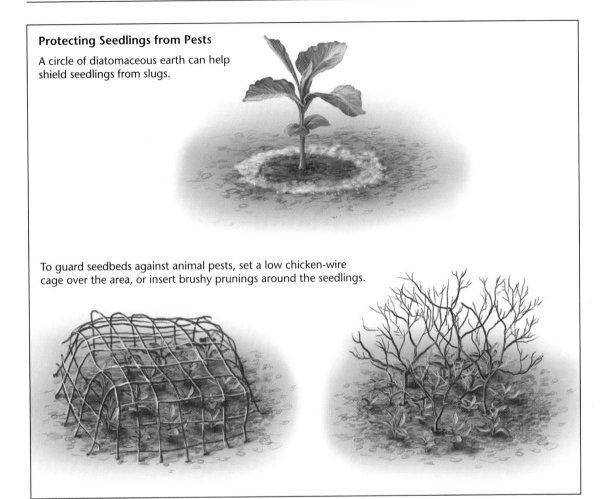

Protecting Seedlings from Pests

A circle of diatomaceous earth can help shield seedlings from slugs.

To guard seedbeds against animal pests, set a low chicken-wire cage over the area, or insert brushy prunings around the seedlings.

running through or digging in seedbeds can quickly wipe out a whole crop of seedlings. To protect your plants, cover the seedbed with wire mesh netting (bend the sides down to make a low cage), or insert brushy prunings into the soil around the seedlings. Remove the covers once seedlings are up and growing strongly, or leave them in to support the growth of slender-stemmed annuals, such as snapdragon *(Antirrhinum majus)*.

CHAPTER 3
MULTIPLYING BY DIVIDING

Division is the fastest, easiest, and most reliable way to propagate a wide variety of perennials and bulbs, as well as some shrubs and vines. Compared to seeds or cuttings, division will generally give you fewer new plants — most clumps will separate into three or more divisions — but each of those pieces will be exact duplicates of the original plant, with the same height, habit, bloom time, and flower color. Plus, most divisions will be large enough to plant directly back into the garden, so they will recover quickly and fill your beds and borders with lush leaves and beautiful flowers.

DECIDING WHEN TO DIVIDE

Plants are surprisingly tough. With proper care, most will tolerate division just about any time of year. But it makes sense to wait until the conditions are ideal so that your divisions will recover as quickly as possible. Dividing plants every

Many perennials, such as these daylilies, are ideal candidates for propagation by division. You can plant the divisions right back into the garden, if you like. If they are small, potting them in containers or pampering them in a nursery bed for a time is best.

few years is a common part of garden maintenance, keeping clumps from getting overcrowded, and you'll get extra plants as a bonus. But you don't have to wait until your plants start having problems to divide them.

How Big Is the Plant?

Within a few years after planting, many clump-forming perennials and bulbs form dense, leafy clumps. Over time, this dense growth can get overcrowded, shading out center shoots and leaving a bare spot in the middle of the clump. The remaining stems may become floppy or spindly, and the plant won't bloom as freely as it did in past years. Crowded growth can also reduce air circulation around leaves and stems, so plants will be more prone to fungal diseases such as powdery mildew, which causes grayish patches on foliage and buds. If you notice these symptoms on any of your perennials or bulbs, plan on dividing them within the next year to help them regain their vigor.

If you wish to divide the clump simply to propagate the plant, you can do it even before the clump starts to look crowded. It's usually best to wait for two years after planting so that the plant has had time to establish and expand a bit, before dividing the first time. After that, you can divide most perennials every two to three years.

What Time of Year Is It?

If your soil is dry enough to dig and is not frozen, you can divide almost any time of year. But if you divide plants while they are actively producing new growth, you'll need to cut the leaves back hard to reduce moisture loss, and the plants will take several weeks or more to settle in and regrow. You'll lose the beauty of the foliage during that time, and the plant may not flower that year either. Midsummer divisions will need careful watering during dry spells, and late fall and winter divisions can be damaged by severe cold or dampness before they can produce new roots.

The ideal time for division is just before a natural growth period. A general rule of thumb is to divide spring-blooming plants from late summer to early fall (they'll start growing new roots then), and fall-blooming plants in late winter or early spring (just as they start into top growth). For summer-blooming plants, divide in either spring or fall. At these times of the year, temperatures tend to be moderate and rainfall more plentiful, encouraging good root growth. The divisions will settle into their new homes quickly and be ready to produce leaves and flowers when conditions are right. Catching plants before a growth period also makes your job easier, since the plump buds or shoots will be easy to see.

DIVIDING CLUMP-FORMING PERENNIALS

Perennials come in an amazing array of heights and growth habits, but for the purposes of propagation, most fall into the category of clump-formers. They may have a fairly solid central crown of tightly packed roots and shoots (as in astilbes), or they may separate naturally into multiple crowns, each with its own roots and top growth (as in chrysanthemums). In other cases, the plants grow outward with creeping aboveground or belowground stems, forming mats of roots and top growth (as in bee balms and lily-of-the-valley). Either kind of clump-forming perennial can be a good candidate for division.

> **TIPS FOR SUCCESS**
>
> **DEALING WITH LARGE PLANTS**
>
> Large clumps of perennials can be a challenge to divide because of their sheer size. If a clump is too large or heavy to lift, don't despair. Simply cut back the top growth and/or brush off as much soil as possible to expose the crown. Use a sharp spade to cut the clump into sections while it is still in the ground, then lift and replant each section separately. This is an especially useful technique for dividing large ornamental grasses, but you will probably need an ax or a mattock to divide the woody crown.

Before you start digging up all your perennials for division, keep in mind that there are a few that usually don't work well with this method. These include perennials that tend to produce brittle roots or long, deep taproots, including baby's-breath *(Gypsophila paniculata),* baptisias *(Baptisia* spp.), gas plant *(Dictamnus albus),* globe thistles *(Echinops* spp.), and lupines *(Lupinus* spp.). Peonies can also be slow to recover and rebloom after division. Whenever possible, it's best to leave these plants in place and propagate them another way, such as by seed or cuttings.

It is possible to divide some clump-forming shrubs, such as barberries *(Berberis* spp.) and spireas *(Spiraea* spp.), the same way you divide perennials. Of course, you'll need much more strength and sturdy tools (such as a heavy spade and loppers or an ax) to dig them up and chop them apart. In most cases, it's easier to just dig up a few rooted shoots from the outside of the clump, as explained in "Removing Offsets, Runners, and Suckers" on page 58. If you do choose to lift a whole shrub for division, follow the same guidelines given here for perennials, but don't cut back the top growth before replanting.

BEST BETS: *Dividing Clumps*

There are far more perennials that you can divide than those you can't. Here's a listing of some of the easiest ones to try, along with the suggested season to divide them in. If you want to divide a plant that isn't on this list, try dividing it in either early spring (as new top growth appears) or late summer.

Divide in Late Winter to Early Spring
Aster spp. Asters.
Astilbe spp. Astilbes.
Chrysanthemum spp. Chrysanthemums.
Phlox spp. Phlox.
Rudbeckia spp. Black-eyed Susans.
Sedum spp. Stonecrops.
Solidago spp. Goldenrods.
Plus warm-season ornamental grasses, such as fountain grass (*Pennisetum* spp.), Japanese blood grass (*Imperata cylindrica* var. *rubra),* and Japanese silver grass *(Miscanthus sinensis).*

Divide in Late Spring Just After Flowering
Epimedium spp. Barrenworts.
Primula spp. Primroses.
Pulmonaria spp. Lungworts.

Late Summer to Early Fall
Achillea spp. Yarrows.
Convallaria majalis. Lily-of-the-valley.
Coreopsis spp. Coreopsis.
Dicentra spp. Bleeding-hearts.
Hemerocallis spp. and hybrids. Daylilies.
Hosta spp. Hostas.
Iris sibirica. Siberian iris.
Mentha spp. Mints.
Monarda spp. Bee balms.
Nepeta spp. Catmints.
Physostegia virginiana. Obedient plant.
Plus cool-season ornamental grasses, such as fescues (*Festuca* spp.).

Consider Replanting Options

The key to success with division is replanting the sections before the roots have a chance to dry out. For that reason, it's smart to gather all the materials you'll need before you start digging up plants. You have three options for handling the divisions: planting in pots, planting in a nursery bed, or planting back into the garden. Each has advantages and disadvantages.

Planting divisions into individual pots takes more work and materials. You'll need several containers: 4-inch pots are fine for small divisions, but 6- to 8-inch pots are more practical for larger pieces. A general growing medium, such as commercial mixes sold for container-grown plants, is also necessary. Add some warm

TROUBLESHOOTING: *Dividing Clumps*

PROBLEM: Divisions fail to recover and grow.

Cause	Solution
Sections did not have roots or buds to start with.	Make sure each section has at least a few roots along with at least one (and ideally two or more) buds or stems.
Divisions dried out before rooting.	Cut back leafy growth before replanting to reduce water loss. Water as needed to keep soil or growing mix evenly moist (but not soggy), especially for the first two to three weeks.
Divisions rotted.	Avoid overwatering or planting in water-logged soil.

PROBLEM: Divisions die over winter.

Cause	Solution
Divisions made too late in season.	Make divisions in late summer or early fall to give divisions a chance to produce new roots before the ground freezes. Protect potted divisions in a cold frame during the winter.
Divisions damaged by frost heaving.	Alternate freezing and thawing can push crowns out of the soil, breaking the tender new roots. Mulching after the soil freezes will help prevent this by keeping the ground evenly cold. If divisions do pop out of ground, push them back in if the soil isn't frozen, or cover them with a pile of mulch until the soil thaws.

water to the mix a few hours before you plan to use it so that it is evenly moist but not soggy. (When you squeeze a handful of mix, the ball left when you open your hand should break apart when you tap it lightly with a finger. If the mix doesn't form a ball, add a bit more water and test again. If the mix stays in a clump, or if water runs out when you squeeze it, add more dry mix, and test again.) After planting, you'll need to water and fertilize potted divisions regularly and, ideally, shelter them in a cold frame. The benefit of this extra effort is that the divisions will recover quickly, with less chance of rotting or drying out. This is especially important if you are making many small divisions from a clump to get as many new plants as possible. Planting divisions in pots is also convenient if you are planning to give some of the new plants away.

Growing divisions in a nursery bed eliminates the need for pots and growing mix. You'll just need to loosen the soil a bit with a spading or hand fork to get it ready for planting. You can leave the divisions in place for several months to a year, until they reach garden size, and they won't need watering as often as potted plants. On the down side, the divisions will be exposed to drying winds, soaking rains, and alternate freezing and thawing, so rooting and recovery may take longer than for pampered container-grown divisions.

Replanting divisions into the garden takes the least work, since you won't have to transplant the divisions again a few months after planting. Plus, it leaves your cold frame or nursery bed space open for more tender seedlings and cuttings. Garden-grown divisions will have little or no shelter, though, so you'll have to pay careful attention to watering to prevent them from drying out. This approach generally works best with medium-size to large divisions with plenty of roots. Prepare the planting site as you would for any new planting, by digging or tilling to loosen the top 8 to 10 inches of soil and smoothing the site with a rake. If you plan to replant the divisions where you dug up the parent clump, add several handfuls of compost (to a small hole) or a mix of compost and topsoil (to a large hole) to enrich the soil before digging and raking.

If the weather has been dry, water thoroughly around the clumps you plan to dig a day or two ahead of time.

Division Techniques

When possible, choose a cool, cloudy day for dividing plants; hot sun and wind can quickly dry out divisions. Lift the clump you want to divide by digging around it with a spading fork, working in a circle 2 to 4 inches out from the perimeter of the clump. Use the fork to lever the clump out of the ground, and shake the excess soil from the clump so that you can see the crown (the point where the roots join the top growth). If you still can't see the buds on the crown, use a hose to rinse as much soil as you can off the clump.

Where the crown is thick and fleshy or rather hard and woody, use a spade or a sharp knife to cut it into several sections. (Try not to cut through any buds.) Separate smaller pieces or loose crowns by breaking and pulling them apart with

Dividing Crown-Forming Plants

To divide crown-forming plants effectively, first dig around the clump with a spading fork and pry it out of the soil. Cut large, tough clumps into quarters with a sharp spade; separate looser clumps with your fingers. Select the youngest, most vigorous portions of the clump for replanting, then replant the divisions into prepared soil.

your fingers. Discard any dead or weak growth from the center, and keep just the vigorous outer growth. Make sure each new division has at least one bud or shoot (ideally more), as well as its own roots.

Dividing a clump into three to five sections, each with several buds or shoots and plenty of roots, will produce pieces large enough for replanting back into the garden. If you are trying to get as many new plants as possible, you can divide down to single crowns so that each piece has only one bud or shoot and some roots. You may be able to get as many as several dozen new plants from an established clump this way. These small divisions will need extra attention to recover and thrive, however, so plant them in individual pots of moist growing mix, or in a nursery bed. Divisions with at least two buds or shoots will reach garden size much more quickly than single divisions.

Caring for New Divisions

If your perennial divisions have leafy growth, cut the tops back to about 3 inches above the roots. This may seem drastic, but removing the leaves will greatly reduce water loss and speed recovery and regrowth. As soon as possible after division, replant the sections at the same depth they grew before (usually with the crown even with the soil surface). Water thoroughly after planting, and again as needed to keep the soil or growing mix evenly moist, especially for the first two to three weeks. Mulching divisions in the garden or nursery bed with an inch or so of shredded bark or chopped leaves will help keep the soil evenly moist and promote rooting.

Set potted divisions in a cold frame or other bright but sheltered spot and water regularly. After four to six weeks, fertilize with liquid fertilizer according to label directions. Leave small divisions in their pots or nursery bed for several months before transplanting them to the garden, either at the end of that growing season or the start of the next.

REMOVING OFFSETS, RUNNERS, AND SUCKERS

Some plants — including perennials and many shrubs — make division so simple that you don't even have to lift them from the ground. These easy-to-propagate plants send out shoots that take root and grow nearby: all you have to do is dig up these rooted plantlets and move them to where you want them. This is an excellent option when you need just one or two new plants.

Identify the Structure

While their value for propagation is similar, offsets, runners, and suckers do look different, and you'll handle them each a little differently.

An offset is a type of sideshoot or branch that develops from the base of the main stem on certain plants. In nature, offsets often become independent of the parent plant by establishing their own root systems. You can take advantage of this by separating and transplanting offsets that have formed their own roots.

Runners are horizontal shoots that grow along the soil surface, with long spaces between the nodes (the points where leaves emerge from the stem). As the runners creep along, the nodes may produce roots and top growth, producing self-supporting new plants that you can dig up and transplant. You can encourage runners to take root by pinning them to the ground or to a pot of moist growing mix sitting near the parent plant. Use a U-shaped piece of wire to keep the runner in contact with the moist soil or mix.

A sucker is a shoot that rises from root tissues below ground, or from stem tissue at the base of the plant. Suckers may appear close to the parent plant or

Encouraging Runners to Root

While most runners will root on their own, you can help speed up the process by pinning them to the ground with a U-shaped piece of wire or an old hairpin. Keep the soil moist to encourage rooting.

BEST BETS: *Dividing Offsets, Runners, and Suckers*

Dividing plants with these specialized structures is especially simple, since the plants do most of the work. All you have to do is wait for the new plantlets to form their own roots; then it's easy to dig them up and move them to a pot, nursery bed, or garden bed. Here are some suggestions of plants you might want to propagate this way.

Offsets
Aloe spp. Aloes.
Ananas spp. Pineapples.
Echeveria spp. Echeverias.
Musa spp. Bananas.
Sempervivum spp. Houseleeks.
Yucca spp. Yuccas.

Runners
Ajuga spp. Ajugas.
Cornus stolonifera. Red-twig dogwood.
Chlorophytum comosum. Spider plant.
Fragaria spp. Strawberries.
Mentha spp. Mints.
Saxifraga stolonifera. Strawberry begonia.

Suckers
Berberis spp. Barberries.
Chaenomeles japonica. Flowering quince.
Deutzia spp. Deutzias.
Hydrangea spp. Hydrangeas.
Kerria japonica. Japanese kerria.
Nandina spp. Nandinas.
Philadelphus spp. Mock oranges.
Rhus spp. Sumacs.
Rosa rugosa. Rugosa rose.
Rubus spp. Raspberries.
Spiraea spp. Spireas.
Syringa spp. Lilacs.

as far as several feet away. When these shoots produce their own roots, it's easy to dig them and move them to another part of your garden. Before digging suckers, however, keep in mind that some plants, including many roses and lilacs, are produced by grafting desirable top growth into the vigorous roots of a closely related (but often less desirable) plant. If you dig a sucker from a grafted plant, that sucker will probably not look like the top growth of the parent plant. In the case of lilac, for instance, the sucker may actually be a privet (*Ligustrum* spp.). If you know a certain plant has been grafted, it's best to just remove and destroy suckers as they appear so that they don't crowd out your desirable plant. If you are not sure whether a plant is grafted or not, closely compare the leaves and stems of the sucker to the parent plant. If they look different, destroy the sucker, and use some other method to propagate the parent plant.

Separating the Plants

Late summer and early spring are good times to separate most offsets, runners, and suckers from their parent plants. If the weather has been dry, water the soil around the plants thoroughly a day or two before division.

The only tools you'll need are possibly a trowel or shovel to dig up the plantlets, and maybe a pair of pruning shears to cut the link between each plantlet and its parent.

Propagating from Suckers

It's easy to propagate plants that produce suckers; simply dig up the rooted plantlets and move them to another part of your garden.

TROUBLESHOOTING: *Dividing Offsets, Runners, and Suckers*

PROBLEM: **Plants fail to recover after you separate them from the parent plant.**

Cause	Solution
Insufficient root system.	Take as many roots as possible with the plantlet when you dig it up. If roots are not prolific, leave it attached to parent for a few more months, or plant it in a pot and care for it as you would a cutting (see chapter 4 for details).
Division dried out.	Water regularly after replanting, especially for the first two to three weeks.

If the plantlets you are separating have many sturdy-looking roots, you can go ahead and plant them right in the garden where you want them to grow. But if there aren't many roots, it's worth planting them in a 4- to 8-inch pot of moist growing mix, or in a nursery bed, for a few months.

If you are dividing a plant with offsets or runners, simply tug on the plantlet gently to make sure it has its own roots (it should resist your pull). If necessary, snip the stem that links the young plant to its parent. Use your fingers or a trowel to dig up the rooted plantlet, and transplant it to a pot, a nursery bed, or the garden.

To see if a sucker is ready to be separated, carefully dig around it, down to the point where it emerged from the parent plant's root or base. If the roots are healthy and prolific, use pruning shears to cut the connection to the parent plant, lift the sucker with as many roots as possible, and transplant it. If there are few roots, either replace the soil and wait a few more months, or remove it, plant it in a pot, and give it some special care (including regular watering and shelter in a cold frame).

If you are moving well-rooted plantlets to another part of the garden, replant and care for them as you would any new plants. Water potted or nursery-bed divisions regularly and allow them to grow for a few months, until fall or the following spring, so that they have a chance to develop a sturdy root system before being transplanted to the garden.

DIVIDING RHIZOMES

Rhizomes are storage structures that grow horizontally at or just below the surface of the soil. These segmented stems have nodes and internodes from which roots grow and lateral branching occurs. Leaves, flowering stems, and upright aboveground shoots also develop from the rhizome or its lateral branches.

Types of Rhizomes

There are two major types of rhizomes: determinate and indeterminate. Determinate rhizomes (such as those of bearded irises) tend to be thick, fleshy, and short, and they end in a flower bud or flowering stalk. A lateral branch forms

Dividing Iris Rhizomes

Lift the rhizomes from the soil with a spading fork, then break or cut young branching rhizomes from the older parent. Inspect for signs of iris borers or soft rot, and destroy infested portions. Trim off any dead growth, and select the youngest portions of the clump for replanting. Discard older portions of the clump. Plant the divisions at their previous depth.

BEST BETS: *Dividing Rhizomes*

Dividing rhizomes is an easy way to expand your collection of some plants. The following rhizome-producing plants are commonly propagated this way.

Bamboos (many species).
Canna spp. Cannas.
Convallaria majalis. Lily-of-the-valley.
Iris hybrids. Bearded irises.
Pachysandra terminalis. Japanese spurge.
Polygonatum spp. Solomon's-seals.
Zingiber officinale. Ginger.

---

from a flowering section, then produces leaves that grow and store food when the flowering stem dies. By the end of the season, this branch forms a flower bud, and the cycle continues. Plants with determinate rhizomes tend to form dense clumps. Indeterminate rhizomes (such as those of lily-of-the-valley) are a bit different, as they keep growing outward from both the tips and side branches. These long, slender rhizomes tend to spread outward, forming extensive patches rather than discrete clumps.

Dividing the Plants

Good times to divide rhizomatous plants include early spring (as new growth appears) and late summer to early fall (when growth is slowing down). With determinate rhizomes, such as bearded irises, it's especially important not to disturb them just after flowering, as they need time to produce new leafy growth and next year's flower buds.

You'll need a minimum of equipment for this propagation technique: just a spading fork to lift the clumps, and perhaps a knife or pruning shears to cut them apart. The divisions will be ready for replanting in the garden, so you won't need to prepare pots or a nursery bed. Just prepare the planting site as you would for any new planting. If you'll be replanting in the same spot, spread an inch or so of compost over the soil and dig it in first.

TROUBLESHOOTING: *Dividing Rhizomes*

PROBLEM: Iris rhizomes eaten by caterpillars or rotted.

Cause	Solution
Bearded irises are susceptible to iris borers, fleshy pink caterpillars that tunnel through the rhizomes. The resulting wounds are then prone to bacterial soft rot, which produces a mushy, foul-smelling rot.	If you find one or two borers or infected spots, cut them out and dust the cut surfaces with sulfur. Discard seriously affected rhizomes, do not compost them.

PROBLEM: Plants did not bloom the season after division.

Cause	Solution
Rhizomes lacked a flower bud.	Divisions of plants with indeterminate rhizomes, such as lily-of-the-valley, may take an extra year to reach flowering size. When dividing determinate rhizomes, such as bearded irises, make sure each new piece has some top growth.

When you are ready to divide plants with rhizomes, simply dig around the clump or patch with a spading fork to lift the rhizomes from the soil. Break or cut off the lateral branches where they join the parent rhizome so that each new piece has at least one bud or shoot. On irises, each new piece will have one or two "fans" of leaves; discard the older rhizomes, which will not bloom again, and cut back the top growth by about half before replanting.

Replant divided rhizomes about 6 inches apart, at the same depth they were growing before. Firm the soil around them, and water thoroughly after replanting. After that, give them the same general care you would give to established plants.

Many lilies produce bulbils where the leaves join the stem. Pot them up in moist growing mix, and keep them in a cold frame or other protected spot. They will take several years to reach blooming size.

DIVIDING BULBS, CORMS, AND TUBEROUS ROOTS

Division is an ideal way to increase your plantings of bulbs, corms, and tuberous roots. With this simple technique, you can quickly and easily propagate daffodils, crocuses, lilies, and many other lovely garden plants. It may take a year or two for the divisions to reach flowering size, but that's much quicker than waiting three to five years for seedlings to mature, and you'll be sure to get exact copies of your favorite flower colors.

Identify the Structure

Bulbs, corms, and tuberous roots all look somewhat different, but they serve the same purpose for the plant — all are food-storage structures.

Bulbs are short and normally globose, tipped with either a growing point or with tissue containing yet-undeveloped flowers. Specialized leaves or leaf bases,

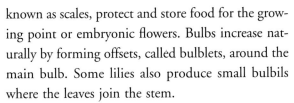
known as scales, protect and store food for the growing point or embryonic flowers. Bulbs increase naturally by forming offsets, called bulblets, around the main bulb. Some lilies also produce small bulbils where the leaves join the stem.

Corms, like bulbs, are swollen underground stems that store food for a new plant. They are often confused with bulbs, but if you dig crocus, gladiolus, or another corm during its dormant period (when it is not actively growing), you will find a new corm growing on top of the previous season's shriveled and depleted corm. Enclosed by dry, leaflike scales, the new corm will have a growing point at the top, lateral buds along the side, and offsets (cormels) attached to it. Removing and replanting these cormels is an easy way to propagate corms.

Tuberous roots, such as those of dahlias, are plump storage roots attached to a central crown, which contains the growing points. Tuberous roots take two growing seasons to mature, and they go dormant when the top growth goes dormant. During their second spring, buds from the crown produce new shoots, nourished by food stored in the old root. During the season, the old root is depleted and new tuberous roots form. You can propagate tuberous-rooted plants by cutting them into sections so that each has at least one bud.

> **Dividing Bulbs**
>
> Dig bulbs after their foliage has turned yellow, and pull them apart to divide them. Replant them twice as deep as their height.

Dividing the Plants

For almost all bulbs and related plants, the best time to divide them is when they are finished flowering and their leaves are dying back. One exception is snowdrops (*Galanthus* spp.); they usually recover best if you divide them while their leaves are still green. Dahlias are another special case; with them, wait until spring. To make it easier to find their buds, press them into 6- to 8-inch pots of moist growing mix, and keep them warm and damp for a week or so. When you can see new growth developing, the roots are ready for division.

BEST BETS: *Dividing Bulbs, Corms, and Tuberous Roots*

Many popular spring- and summer-flowering bulbs, corms, and tuberous roots are easy to divide. Here's a listing of some of the most popular candidates for this type of propagation.

Bulbs
Allium spp. Ornamental onions.
Galanthus spp. Snowdrops.
Lilium spp. and hybrids. Lilies.
Leucojum spp. Snowflakes.
Muscari spp. Grape hyacinths.
Narcissus spp. and hybrids. Daffodils.
Scilla spp. Squills.
Tulipa spp. and hybrids. Tulips.

Corms
Crocus spp. and hybrids. Crocus.
Gladiolus spp. and hybrids. Gladiolus.

Tuberous Roots
Dahlia hybrids. Dahlias.

Propagating Lilies from Bulblets and Bulbils

Dig lilies in fall, after the stem has yellowed, and pick off the small bulblets that have formed along the stem between the parent bulb and the soil surface. Plant the bulblets in pots or in a nursery bed. Bulbils, found along the stems, can be picked and potted up as well.

Bulbil

Bulblet

To divide bulbs and corms, you won't need any special tools: just a spading or hand fork to lift the clumps. A sharp, clean knife is necessary for dividing dahlia roots. In most cases, you can replant divisions outdoors, into the garden (for large offsets) or into a nursery bed (for smaller divisions). If you are returning the bulbs to the same spot, dig a few handfuls of compost into the area before replanting; otherwise, prepare the site as you would for any new planting. If the divisions are small, such as many lily bulblets and bulbils and gladiolus cormels, they'll benefit from some special care, so be prepared to plant them in 4-inch pots of moist growing mix.

When the leaves of bulbs and corms start to turn yellow, use a spading or hand fork to dig them up. Remember that large bulbs, such as lilies, may be 8 or more inches below the surface, so dig deeply. Lift the clumps and shake off the excess soil.

With most bulbs and crocuses, break the clumps apart to separate the offsets, and pull off the top growth. You can replant them all where you want them to grow, or just replant the largest offsets and grow the smaller ones in a nursery bed for a year or two, until they reach flowering size and are ready to return to the garden. Plant offsets at the same depth they were growing before.

When you dig up lily bulbs, you'll see small bulblets have formed along the stem between the parent bulb and the soil surface. Pull them off and plant them at a depth about twice their diameter, either in a nursery bed or in a pot of moist growing mix. (Plant the parent bulb back in the garden after trimming off the old stem.) If your lilies produce bulbils in the joints where the leaves meet the stem, you can pick off these small dark minibulbs in late summer, when they loosen, and handle them the same way as bulblets.

To propagate gladiolus, dig up the corms in fall, as the foliage yellows. Break off the old shriveled corms and discard them, and pick off the small cormels that have

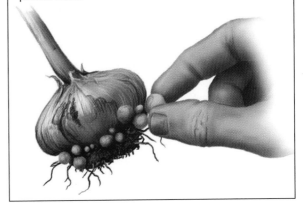

Dividing Gladiolus Corms

Dig gladiolus corms after the foliage has turned yellow. Discard the withered old corm, and pick off the small cormels that have formed around the base of the parent corm.

formed around the plump new corm. Store the corms and cormels in a cool, dry place until spring. Plant the full-size corms in the garden, and plant the cormels 1 to 2 inches deep in a nursery bed or a pot of moist growing mix. (If the cormels seem very hard and dry in spring, try soaking them in cool water overnight, then mix them with moist peat moss. Keep them moist until roots start to appear, then plant immediately.)

Divide dahlias in the spring (at the end of their winter storage in northern zones). Cut the clusters apart by slicing carefully through the crown so that each new piece has at least one bud. Plant the sections in pots of moist growing mix,

Dividing Dahlias

Using a sharp, clean knife, cut the clump into sections, so that each has at least one root and part of the crown. Dust the cuts with sulfur to prevent fungal diseases, then plant the divisions in pots or directly into the garden (after the last frost).

TROUBLESHOOTING: *Dividing Bulbs, Corms, and Tuberous Roots*

Problem: Divisions grow but do not flower the following year.

Cause	Solution
Divisions need more time to mature.	Offset from bulbs and corms often need an additional year or two to reach flowering size. Very small offsets, such as bulblets, bulbils, and cormels, may take three years or more.

Problem: Divisions do not regrow the following year.

Cause	Solution
Divisions rotted.	Improve soil drainage; avoid overwatering. To discourage disease development, dust cut surfaces of divisions with powdered sulfur before planting.

---

or plant them directly out in the garden. Small roots may produce only foliage the first year, but they will flower if you replant them the following year.

Caring for Divisions

Divisions replanted in the garden or a nursery bed need minimal aftercare: just water during dry spells in fall to encourage good root growth. Transplant those growing in a nursery bed to the garden after a year or two.

If you've planted small offsets in pots, cover the growing mix with a 1/4- to 1/2-inch layer of fine, washed gravel (such as that sold for use in aquariums). This will help to keep the growing mix evenly moist and prevent it from crusting over. Set the pots in a cold frame, and water as needed to prevent the mix from drying out completely. The fall after potting, transplant the bulbs to individual pots or to a nursery bed to grow to flowering size.

In cold climates, don't forget to bring developing gladiolus cormels indoors in fall for winter storage, as you would for full-size corms. Bring dahlia root clusters indoors, too. Store gladiolus and dahlias in barely moist vermiculite or sawdust at 40° to 45°F.

CHAPTER 4
TAKING CUTTINGS

Plants have an amazing ability to regenerate themselves. From a small section of stem, leaf, or root, they can grow a whole new root system and new leafy growth. You can take advantage of this ability to propagate a wide range of annuals, perennials, herbs, houseplants, shrubs, vines, and trees.

Unlike seeds, which can produce variable seedlings, with just a few exceptions cuttings will give you an exact copy, or clone, of the parent plant. Cuttings can also mature faster than seedlings, so they will reach full size more quickly and bloom sooner. This technique limits your options for growing new plants a bit more than seed does, as you need access to an existing plant for the cutting material, but it's a great way to increase the stock of plants you already have, for filling new gardens or expanding existing plantings.

DECIDING WHEN TO TAKE CUTTINGS

The ideal timing for taking cuttings depends on the plants you want to propagate. With indoor plants, you can gather cuttings year-round. With outdoor

Some cuttings, including a variety of begonias, are so eager to root that all they need is a jar of fresh water. A wide variety of annuals, perennials, bulbs, herbs, shrubs, vines, and trees are easy to propagate from cuttings.

plants, timing is more important. Some cuttings root best while they're growing, some root best when gathered during the dormant season, and still others can root either way. Here's an overview of your best options for different seasons:

Late fall to midwinter: Take stem cuttings of deciduous shrubs, vines, and trees, as well as needle-leaved evergreens.

Late winter to early spring: Some perennials, shrubs, vines, and trees can be propagated by root cuttings taken at this season.

Spring and summer: Some houseplants and perennials can be propagated by leaf cuttings taken at this season.

Midsummer to late summer: Take stem cuttings of annuals, perennials, and herbs, as well as of deciduous shrubs and trees and broad-leaved evergreens.

CUTTINGS FROM ANNUALS AND PERENNIALS

A wide range of annuals and perennials that have leafy, branching stems — including many popular herbs — can be propagated from soft-stemmed cuttings. You will need to use division or seeds to reproduce plants that grow from basal rosettes, such as columbines (*Aquilegia* spp.), daylilies (*Hemerocallis* spp.), irises (*Iris* spp.), ornamental grasses, and torch lilies (*Kniphofia* spp.).

Mid- to late summer is a great time to gather cuttings of many annuals and perennials. Summer temperatures are usually ideal for rooting, so you won't need to provide supplemental heat. There also are plenty of stems to choose from, and growth has slowed down somewhat, so the leaves have "hardened" a bit and aren't as prone to water loss. A few perennials may also root well or better from cuttings taken earlier in the season, from newly emerging shoots in mid- to late spring. If you don't have luck rooting certain plants from midsummer cuttings, gather cuttings earlier the following year.

TIPS FOR SUCCESS

TAKE CUTTINGS FOR OVERWINTERING

Cuttings provide a handy method for bringing annuals or tender perennials indoors for the winter. By taking cuttings in late summer, you can enjoy your favorite colors or flower forms year after year. Cuttings eliminate the need to dig up the whole plant and make room for it indoors. Instead, just pot up a few cuttings and grow them on a windowsill or under lights for the winter. Set them outdoors again the following spring. In late winter, if you like, you can take more cuttings from your overwintered plants to fill a garden bed or share with friends.

By taking and rooting cuttings of plants such as these coleus, you can make exact duplicates, or clones, of them to keep favorite foliage patterns or flower colors from year to year. This group of plants is 'Wizard Mix', which is a strain that can also be grown from seed.

Getting Ready

The trick to success with soft-stemmed cuttings is to keep them from drying out before they can establish a new root system. This means that you'll need to gather and plant them quickly. You can minimize the time between gathering and planting by preparing all of your materials ahead of time. For collecting the cuttings, you'll need a sharp, clean pair of pruning or garden shears, and a large plastic bag to gather them in. For planting, you'll need pots (clean 4-inch plastic pots are great for cuttings) and some flats to carry the pots in.

You'll also need a growing medium with a good balance of aeration and moisture retention. A mix of equal parts peat moss and perlite works well for a wide variety of cuttings. You could also try vermiculite by itself, or mixed with an equal amount of perlite. Some gardeners get good results with straight perlite, although

Keeping Humidity High

Soft-stemmed cuttings are prone to wilting, so it's critical to keep humidity high to prevent water loss from the leaves. Enclose them in a propagator with a plastic dome, a clear plastic sweater box with a lid, or a homemade frame draped with clear plastic.

BEST BETS: Annuals and Perennials

Annuals and perennials generally root quickly and easily from cuttings.
The following are some of the easiest to root from cuttings.

Centranthus ruber. Red valerian.

Chelone spp. Turtleheads.

Chrysanthemum spp. Chrysanthemums.

Coleus blumei. Coleus.

Dianthus spp. Pinks.

Iberis sempervirens. Perennial candytuft.

Impatiens spp. Impatiens.

Lamium spp. Dead nettles.

Linum spp. Flaxes.

Melissa officinalis. Lemon balm.

Mentha spp. Mints.

Monarda spp. Bee balms.

Nepeta spp. Catmints.

Pelargonium spp. Zonal and scented geraniums.

Penstemon spp. Beardtongues.

Phlox spp. Phlox.

Salvia spp. Sages, especially frost-tender species.

Sedum spp. Stonecrops.

Thymus spp. Thymes.

Verbena spp. Verbenas.

the coarse grade may not hold enough water for good rooting; try medium-grade
perlite if you can find it.

To keep humidity high around your cuttings, you'll also need to prepare
some kind of enclosure for them. (High humidity reduces moisture loss during
the crucial period before the cuttings have developed a root system to replace lost
moisture.) You'll often see recommendations to cover individual pots with upside
down plastic bags, but this system can be more trouble than it's worth. It's tricky
to find the right size bag — one that's not too large and floppy or too small and
cramped — and it's often difficult to get the bag over the cuttings or remove it
without bumping them. Unless you are just planting one pot of cuttings (which
is kind of like eating just one potato chip), it is much easier to use a more rigid
enclosure that can hold several pots at once. Many garden-supply catalogs sell
propagators that are specifically designed for this purpose, but you can easily
make your own from a clear plastic sweater box that's about 8 inches deep. Alternately, you could construct a light wooden or PVC frame that's an inch or so
longer and wider than a flat, and 8 to 12 inches high. Place your pots of cuttings
into the flat, place the frame over them, drape a large sheet of plastic (such as a
dry-cleaning bag) over the frame, and tuck in the edges.

Taking Cuttings of Annuals and Perennials

Snip off healthy shoots roughly 3 to 4 inches long, making the bottom cut just below a node (the point where leaves join the stem).

Remove the leaves from the bottom half of each cutting.

Insert the cuttings about halfway into a pot of moist growing medium after making a guide hole with a pencil. After planting, lightly firm the medium around the cuttings and water well.

Gathering Soft-Stemmed Cuttings

Before going out to collect your cuttings, fill your containers with whatever medium you've chosen to within $\frac{1}{2}$ to $\frac{1}{4}$ inch of the rim. Water the pots thoroughly and set them aside to drain.

Gather cuttings early in the day, while the stems are full of moisture. Cuttings from wilted or water-stressed plants are much less likely to recover and root well. In fact, if your weather has been dry, it's smart to water thoroughly the day before gathering your cuttings.

Choose cutting material from strong-looking growth, with leaves that have fully expanded and growth that has hardened a bit. Avoid shoots that are spindly or that are growing especially rapidly. To judge if the growth is at the best stage for cutting, try bending one of the plant's stems firmly. If it snaps off cleanly, it's a good time to collect cuttings. If the growth just bends, it's too soft; if it crushes or only partially breaks, it's on the old side and may be slow to root. Snip off 2- to 6-inch shoots with a sharp, clean pair of pruning or garden shears. Make sure each shoot has at least two nodes (the joints where the leaves or leaf pairs emerge from the stem). Gather the shoots from different areas on the plant; otherwise it will look lopsided for the rest of the growing season. If you need many cuttings, it's smart to plan ahead and grow a special "stock" plant in a nursery bed or other out-of-the-way spot. That way, you can take as many cuttings as you need without worrying about the plant's appearance.

Collect your cuttings in a large plastic bag to prevent them from drying out, and keep them out of direct sun. As soon as you have all the cuttings you need, take them indoors and prepare them for planting. If you can't plant them immediately, wrap them in a moist paper towel, and keep them in the plastic bag in a cool, shady spot until you are ready for them.

Planting Soft-Stemmed Cuttings

Using a sharp, clean pair of shears or a utility knife, trim each shoot to its final cutting size. Most soft-stemmed cuttings are 2 to 4 inches long. Whenever possible, trim each cutting so that there are at least two nodes left, and make the bottom cut just below a node. Trim the leaves off of the bottom half of the cutting, and remove any flowers or flower buds. Use a pencil to poke a hole in the growing medium, then insert the cutting about halfway into the medium, to just below the lowest leaves. Push the medium back around the stem to support the cutting. Repeat with the remaining cuttings, spacing them 1 to 4 inches apart. The cuttings shouldn't touch, so if the leaves are large, either space the cuttings farther apart or trim their leaves slightly (by no more than one-half). A 4-inch pot usually holds three to nine cuttings, depending on their size. Different plants root at different rates, so it's best to use separate pots for each different plant.

TROUBLESHOOTING: *Annual and Perennial Cuttings*

PROBLEM: Cuttings wilt.

Cause	Solution
Air too dry around cuttings.	Enclose potted cuttings in a commercial propagator, clear plastic sweater box, or homemade plastic frame to keep humidity high; mist with a hand mister, if needed. Water before growing medium dries out.
Temperature too hot.	Set covered cuttings where they'll get plenty of light but no direct sun.

PROBLEM: Cuttings do not root.

Cause	Solution
Cuttings water-stressed.	Gather cuttings early in the day. Water parent plant the day before if weather has been dry. Collect, prepare, and plant cuttings quickly to keep them from drying out. Cover cuttings to maintain humidity around leaves.
Temperature too hot or cool.	Keep air temperature between 65° and 75°F and the medium at 70° to 75°F; use a heating mat if necessary.
Cuttings taken at wrong time of year.	Try taking cuttings at a different time, perhaps 2 to 3 weeks earlier or later.

PROBLEM: Cuttings rot.

Cause	Solution
Medium too wet.	Use containers with drainage holes, and don't allow water to collect in the flat the pots are sitting in. Water sparingly.
Medium contaminated.	Try again with fresh growing medium; do not reuse medium for planting more cuttings. Remove dead leaves and cuttings as soon as you see them. Water with fresh tap water, not water that's been stored outdoors.

PROBLEM: Cuttings die soon after potting.

Cause	Solution
Transplanted too soon.	Leave in cutting pot a week or so longer next time to allow better root development.
Lack of nutrients.	A week or so after transplanting, start fertilizing with a liquid fertilizer, following the directions on the label.

Label each pot with the name of the plant and the date. After planting, water all cuttings thoroughly.

Now, set your cuttings in ideal conditions for rooting. They need warmth, light, and high humidity. The ideal air temperature is 65° to 75°F, and the growing medium should be a steady 70° to 75°F. If necessary, you can set potted cuttings on a heated propagating mat to keep the growing medium evenly warm. To keep the humidity high around the leaves, put the potted cuttings in the enclosure you prepared (as described in "Getting Ready" on page 75). Then place the cover on the propagator or sweater box, or set the plastic tent over the flat of cuttings. Ample but not intense light is also important. Direct sun can quickly dry out tender cuttings. Outdoors, set covered cuttings at the base of a north-facing wall or in a spot that's lightly shaded all day by trees or shrubs. Cuttings can also root well under fluorescent lights; use the same setup you'd use for starting seeds indoors.

Caring for Soft-Stemmed Cuttings

Within a day, condensation should build up on the inside of the propagation enclosure. If not, water again thoroughly. Otherwise, leave the cuttings covered and water only when the condensation thins or disappears; don't let the cutting pots sit in water. Remove the cover for an hour or so two or three times a week to allow some air circulation around the leaves. If you have your cuttings on a heated propagation mat, use a soil thermometer to monitor the temperature of the medium. High temperatures can damage the stem bases and reduce the chance of successful rooting. Remove any dropped leaves or obviously dead cuttings immediately to discourage diseases from developing.

Most soft-stemmed plants start rooting in two to five weeks. Try to resist the urge to check for roots until you see the cuttings producing new growth, then tug lightly on the stems. When the cuttings feel firmly anchored in the medium, they are ready to be transplanted to a pot. Gradually remove or open the enclosure over several days to increase ventilation and decrease humidity. This will help the new growth harden off and reduce the chance of wilting.

When you are ready to pot up your cuttings, gather some 2½- to 3-inch pots and some premoistened growing mix. You can use larger pots if you have large cuttings or if you want to grow several cuttings together to create a bushy plant

Root Cuttings in Water

Some plants are so ready to grow that you can root them in a glass of water on your windowsill. Simply fill a drinking glass or wide-mouthed jar with several inches of fresh, tepid tap water, and lay a piece of chicken wire or plastic mesh over the top. Gather your cuttings as described in "Gathering Soft-Stemmed Cuttings" on page 78. Carefully remove the leaves from the bottom half of each cutting, and insert the cuttings through the covering. Make sure that at least the bottom inch or so of each stem is in the water. The leaves shouldn't be in or touching the water, as they'll be prone to rot.

Set the cuttings where they will get bright but indirect light. Every few days, dump out the old water and add fresh tepid water to prevent the buildup of harmful bacteria. After a week or two, you'll see roots starting to develop. After another two to three weeks, move the cuttings into individual pots of growing mix, as you would other kinds of rooted cuttings.

A few good candidates to try this way include basil, coleus *(Coleus blumei),* impatiens *(Impatiens* spp.), oleander *(Nerium oleander),* sweet potatoes *(Ipomoea batatas),* and willows *(Salix* spp.).

Rooting Cuttings in Water

Add several inches of water to a wide-mouthed jar or glass. Place a piece of screen or mesh over the mouth to support the cuttings. Remove the leaves from the bottom half of the cuttings, and insert them so that the bottom few inches of the stems are submerged.

Potting Up Rooted Cuttings

First, fill several pots about halfway with moist growing mix.

Gently dig out the rooted cuttings, and separate them with your fingers.

Transfer one cutting at a time to its own pot, spreading its roots out over the growing mix. Add more mix to evenly cover the roots. Lightly tap the base of the pot against a hard surface a few times to settle the mix around the roots.

Water thoroughly and set potted cuttings in a shady spot. Mist with a hand sprayer a few times a day for the first few days after transplanting.

quickly. Otherwise, it's best to make the first planting into pots that are just large enough to hold the existing roots; you can transplant again later as needed.

Fill each pot about halfway with moist growing mix. Gently dig out the rooted cuttings and separate them with your fingers. Hold a cutting in the center of a pot so that the point where the roots emerge from the stem is 1/4 to 1/2 inch below the top of the pot. With your other hand, scoop more moist mix around the roots, until the mix is just below the rim of the pot. Lightly tap the base of the pot against a hard surface twice to settle the mix around the roots, then water thoroughly. Set potted cuttings in a shady spot and mist them a few times with a hand sprayer each day for two or three days to help them recover; then move them to their preferred light conditions and water and fertilize as usual.

CUTTINGS FROM SHRUBS, VINES, AND TREES

Cuttings from woody-stemmed plants tend to be slower to root than soft-stemmed cuttings — especially when you take them during the dormant season (while the plant isn't producing new growth). On the plus side, these cuttings are easy to prepare and require little or no special equipment. Woody cuttings are also less touchy about water loss, so they don't need as much careful attention.

The techniques and timing you'll use for propagating woody plants will vary, depending on the particular plants you're working with. Deciduous shrubs, vines, and trees usually root from semiripe cuttings collected in mid- to late summer or from hardwood cuttings collected in late fall to midwinter, after the leaves have dropped but before the buds start to grow again. Narrow-leaved evergreens — such as junipers (*Juniperus* spp.) and yews (*Taxus* spp.) — tend to root best in late fall or early winter, after a few frosts. And for broad-leaved evergreens, such as rhododendrons (*Rhododendron* spp.) and hollies (*Ilex* spp.), you'll generally get good results by collecting cuttings in mid- to late summer, soon after they have finished a new flush of growth.

If you are taking semiripe cuttings of deciduous woody shrubs, vines, or trees (collected in mid- to late summer), give them the same special attention you'd give to soft-stemmed plants. Have a sweater box or other enclosure ready for them, and collect and stick the cuttings in the same way you would soft-stemmed cuttings. See "Cuttings from Annuals and Perennials" on page 74 for details.

Getting Ready for Hardwood Cuttings

Cuttings you collect from late summer to midwinter won't dry out as fast as soft-stemmed cuttings, so you don't have to work with them as quickly. To gather hardwood cuttings, you'll need a sharp, clean pair of pruning shears. If you are working with hardwood cuttings of dormant deciduous plants, you can plant them directly into an outdoor nursery bed. Or you can plant both hardwood and evergreen cuttings in 3½- or 4-inch plastic pots. For potted cuttings, you'll also need at least one flat to carry the pots in, as well as a growing medium with a good balance of aeration and moisture retention. A mix of equal parts peat moss and perlite works well for many woody-stemmed cuttings. If you can find a source for medium-grade perlite, you could use that alone instead. (The coarse grade may not hold enough water for good rooting.)

BEST BETS: *Shrubs, Vines, and Trees*

Woody-stemmed plants can be more challenging to root than annuals and perennials, but with the proper timing and technique, you can still expect good results. Here's an overview of some shrubs, vines, and trees that are relatively easy to grow from cuttings. Try these for a start, then experiment with others.

Deciduous Shrubs, Vines, and Trees
Abelia spp. Abelias.
Deutzia spp. Deutzias.
Forsythia spp. Forsythias.
Hydrangea spp. Hydrangeas.
Kerria japonica. Japanese kerria.
Lagerstroemia spp. Crape myrtles.
Ligustrum spp. Privets.
Lonicera spp. Honeysuckles.
Philadelphus coronarius. Mock orange.
Rosa spp. Roses.
Salix spp. Willows.
Spiraea spp. Spireas.
Syringa spp. Lilacs.

Weigela florida. Weigela.
Wisteria spp. Wisterias.

Broad-leaved Evergreens
Camellia spp. Camellias.
Euonymus spp. Euonymus.
Ilex spp. Hollies.
Rhododendron spp. Rhododendrons.

Needle-leaved Evergreens
Chamaecyparis spp. False cypresses.
Juniperus horizontalis. Creeping juniper.
Taxus spp. Yews.
Thuja spp. Arborvitae.

Taking Deciduous Hardwood Cuttings

After leaves have dropped, choose healthy, moderately vigorous, pencil-thick shoots, and cut stems to about 10 inches long.

Trim an inch or two off the tip, and cut the rest of the stem into 4- to 8-inch lengths, with at least two buds on each length.

Make a straight cut above a bud at the top end of each piece, and a sloping cut below the bud at the base.

Plant hardwood cuttings immediately in mild-winter areas, but in northern zones store bundles of them in boxes of moist vermiculite in an unheated room, or buried outdoors.

Plant in early spring. Plant hardwood cuttings outdoors in moist, well-prepared soil deep enough to cover all but the top one or two buds.

Since hardwood cuttings don't have leafy growth, you don't need to worry about keeping them in high-humidity conditions. Evergreen cuttings do have leaves, so providing a humid environment will help reduce moisture stress and promote rooting. Prepare the same kind of enclosure you'd use for cuttings of annuals and perennials.

Gathering Hardwood Cuttings

Wait for two to three weeks after the plants have dropped their leaves to collect hardwood cuttings. You'll usually get best results from wood of the current year's growth (first-year shoots), although second-year or older growth may root as well. Look for healthy, moderately vigorous shoots that are about as thick as a pencil. Avoid lanky stems or crowded, spindly interior shoots. Cut stems at least 8 inches long or longer (you may be able to get several smaller cuttings from one long stem piece), and trim an inch or two off the tip.

Take cuttings of broad-leaved evergreens after a flush of new growth has finished and the stems are starting to harden. Take 4 to 6 inches of the tip growth from healthy, moderately vigorous shoots.

When gathering cuttings from needle-leaved evergreens, choose healthy tip growth. Cut 3 to 5 inches back from the tip so that there's $1/4$ to $1/2$ inch of brown stem along with the green-stemmed tip growth.

Planting Deciduous Hardwood Cuttings

Trim the leafless stems of hardwood cuttings into 4- to 8-inch lengths, with at least two buds on each length. Make a straight cut about $1/2$ inch above a bud at the top end of each piece (the end that was closest to the shoot tip), and a sloping cut about $1/2$ inch below the bud at the base. It's important to plant the cuttings right-side up so that this system will help you keep track of which end is which. Cuttings planted upside down won't root.

If your winters are relatively mild (roughly Zone 6 or south), you can plant hardwood cuttings outdoors immediately. Treating them with rooting hormone before planting can encourage rooting; see "Tips for Rooting Difficult Cuttings" on page 91 for more information. Insert them vertically into moistened, loose soil, leaving only one or two buds aboveground, and lightly firm the soil around the cuttings. Mulch the soil around the cuttings after the ground freezes to

prevent rapid thawing and refreezing, which can damage the tender new roots that are developing.

Where winters are long and cold, it's best to store your hardwood cuttings for early spring planting. Besides guarding them from extreme cold, the storage process promotes the growth of protective callus tissue at the base of each cutting, increasing the chance of successful rooting. After treating your cuttings with rooting hormone, gather them into bundles with the top ends all facing one direction, and secure them with rubber bands. To keep them cool and moist over the winter, you could bury them outdoors in a well-drained spot filled with sandy soil, sand, or sawdust. Place the bundles horizontally, 6 to 8 inches deep, or vertically, with their tops down and their basal ends 3 to 4 inches below the soil surface. Alternately, you could store them in boxes of moist sand, sawdust, or peat moss in an unheated room or garage or in your refrigerator. In early spring, plant your stored cuttings outdoors in moist, well-prepared soil, deep enough to cover all but the top one or two buds. Space them roughly 4 to 6 inches apart.

Planting Evergreen Cuttings

Cuttings from broad- or needle-leaved evergreens need a bit more attention for best results. On broad-leaved evergreen cuttings, remove the leaves from the bottom half of the cutting. (To save space, you may also choose to trim the remaining leaves in half on large-leaved plants, such as rhododendrons.) Remove the leaves from the bottom 2 to 3 inches of narrow-leaved evergreen cuttings.

Treating evergreen cuttings with rooting hormone before planting can help encourage root formation; see "Tips for Rooting Difficult Cuttings" on page 91. Insert the cuttings almost halfway into pots of moist growing mix, to just below the lowest leaf or leaves. Allow enough space between cuttings so that their foliage doesn't touch. (A 4-inch pot usually holds three to six evergreen cuttings.) Water the medium to settle it around the cuttings, and allow the pots to drain.

If you have a greenhouse or a spot indoors where you can provide high light, high humidity, and bottom heat (to keep the growing medium at 75° to 80°F), placing the cuttings in these conditions can hasten rooting. Otherwise, set the pots in a well-lighted and well-protected cold frame for the winter. Keep the growing medium evenly moist through the rooting process.

Taking Cuttings of Broad-Leaved Evergreens

Collect 4- to 6-inch pieces of tip growth after a flush of new growth has finished and the stems are starting to harden. Remove the leaves from the bottom half of the cutting, and cut back the remaining foliage of large-leaved cuttings by half. Insert cuttings almost halfway into pots of moist growing medium, to just below the lowest leaf or leaves.

Aftercare

Cuttings from woody plants may take several months to a year to root. Summer cuttings of deciduous shrubs, vines, and trees are usually the quickest to get started. For general care, follow the guidelines given in "Caring for Soft-Stemmed Cuttings" on page 81. Instead of transplanting the rooted cuttings soon after you remove their enclosure, however, set them in a sheltered corner or cold frame for the winter. When you see new growth start in spring, fertilize the cuttings. Two to four weeks later, transplant them to individual pots, as you would annual or perennial cuttings. When the cuttings are well rooted in their pots (usually by

TROUBLESHOOTING: *Shrub, Vine, and Tree Cuttings*

PROBLEM: Cuttings don't produce roots.

Cause	Solution
Cuttings are naturally slow to produce roots.	Try applying rooting hormone and/or wounding the stems before planting.
Cuttings died over winter.	Avoid overwatering. Mulch hardwood cuttings after ground freezes. Ventilate or protect cold frame as needed to avoid overheating or freezing.

PROBLEM: Hardwood cuttings produce top growth but no roots.

Cause	Solution
Cuttings taken at the wrong time (too close to spring).	Gather cuttings earlier next year (late fall to midwinter).

PROBLEM: Cuttings rot.

Cause	Solution
Growing medium or soil too wet.	Avoid overwatering. Plant in well-drained soil outdoors. Don't let pots stand in water.
Growing medium contaminated.	Don't reuse growing medium; try fresh medium next time. Remove dead leaves and cuttings as you see them. Water with tap water, not water stored outdoors.

mid- to late summer), transplant them to a nursery bed. Move them to your garden the following spring or fall.

Hardwood cuttings growing outdoors may be big enough to move to the garden after one growing season (in the fall after planting), but it's generally best to leave them undisturbed for an extra growing season to make sure their roots are well established.

To judge the progress of evergreen cuttings, look to see if roots are visible through the drainage holes on the bottoms of the pots. Transplant rooted cuttings to a nursery bed in late summer or fall, and allow them to grow for a year or two before moving them to your garden. If the potted cuttings haven't yet rooted but still look healthy, hold them over winter in a cold frame and transplant them to your nursery bed the following spring.

TIPS FOR ROOTING DIFFICULT CUTTINGS

With good timing and careful attention, many kinds of cuttings will produce roots readily. But some plants — particularly those with woody stems — can be slow to root without some extra encouragement. For some of these, dusting or dipping their cuttings in rooting hormones can provide the boost they need to succeed. For others, simply scratching or wounding the stem can be enough.

Try Rooting Hormones

One of the greatest advances made in the propagation of plants from cuttings was the discovery of natural and artificial root-promoting substances. When produced naturally within the plant, these substances are called hormones. Synthetic root-producing substances are technically not hormones, but they are generally referred to that way. They won't promote rooting on plants that normally wouldn't root, even under the best conditions. But for most plants, hormones will hasten the formation of roots, increase the percentage of cuttings that do root, and increase the number, quality, and overall uniformity of the roots that develop.

One of the most commonly used synthetic rooting hormones is indolebutyric acid (IBA). It is available in a powder form, which you can use directly on cuttings, and in a liquid form, which you'll need to dilute in water to get the desired concentration. Some powders also include a fungicide to reduce the chance of disease problems while cuttings are rooting. Beginners generally find hormone powders easier to use, since there is no mixing. (As you gain experience, you may want to experiment with liquids, since you can dilute them to different strengths for different plants.)

Dipping cuttings directly into the hormone's container could contaminate the material with disease-causing organisms, so separate only enough of the powder to treat the cuttings at hand. You won't need much: an amount about the size of a dime can treat roughly half a dozen cuttings. Discard the unused amount when you are finished.

To apply hormone powder, make a fresh cut at the base of the cutting or press it against a damp sponge to moisten the base. Dip just the base of the cutting in the powder, and roll it to ensure the entire base is covered. Gently tap the cutting against something solid to remove excess powder, which could harm the cutting, then plant it as you would an untreated cutting.

Wounding Woody Stems

Cuttings of some woody-stemmed plants — especially evergreens — also benefit from a technique known as wounding. Good candidates to try include arborvitae (*Thuja* spp.), hollies (*Ilex* spp.), junipers (*Juniperus* spp.), magnolias (*Magnolia* spp.), and rhododendrons (*Rhododendron* spp.).

To wound a cutting, use a clean knife or razor blade to make a 1-inch-long vertical slice, through the bark and into the wood, on one or both sides of the basal end. Alternately, you can remove a thin, shallow slice of bark from the same area. After wounding, treat the cutting with rooting hormone (make sure to get powder on the whole wounded area) and plant as usual. Wounded cuttings are able to absorb more water and rooting hormone, and they generally produce a larger, better-balanced root system from the cut areas.

Wounding Cuttings

With a sharp knife, make a 1-inch-long vertical slice, through the bark and into the wood, on one side of the basal end of a prepared cutting. Dust the cut surfaces with rooting hormone before planting.

CUTTINGS FROM LEAVES

In some cases, you can get a whole new plant from just a small section of leaf. This type of propagation works best on a few special plants, mostly indoor plants. But it's a handy technique to know if you want to increase your stock of some favorite houseplants. The best time to take leaf cuttings is generally spring and summer, soon after the leaves are fully expanded but while they are still green and vigorous. Rapidly growing leaves are quick to wilt, and older, yellowing leaves often root poorly.

Gathering and Planting Leaf Cuttings

The way you'll collect and prepare leaf cuttings will vary, depending on the particular plant you're propagating. Since all leaf cuttings are susceptible to drying out, however, you'll need to be ready for planting as soon as you take them. Gather your materials the same way you would for soft-stemmed cuttings; see "Getting Ready" on page 75. As with soft-stemmed cuttings, a mix of equal parts peat moss and perlite works well for leaf cuttings.

On plants with long, narrow leaves, such as cape primroses and snake plants, use a sharp, clean knife to remove a suitable leaf — one that is fully expanded,

---

BEST BETS: *Leaf Cuttings*

If you'd like to give leaf cuttings a try, some good candidates are listed below. One thing to keep in mind is that leaf cuttings from some variegated plants, such as variegated snake plant (*Sansevieria trifasciata* 'Laurentii'), may actually produce all-green plants. If you want to reproduce these plants exactly, striped leaves and all, try division instead.

Begonia masoniana and *B. rex.*
   Begonias (some).
Crassula ovata. Jade plant.
Echeveria spp. Echeverias.
Saintpaulia hybrids. African violets.

Sansevieria spp. Snake plants.
Sedum spp. Stonecrops.
Sinningia speciosa. Gloxinias.
Streptocarpus hybrids. Cape primroses.
Tolmeia menziesii. Piggy-back plant.

Rex begonias are one of the houseplants that can be propagated from leaf cuttings. Here a colorful new plantlet of rex begonia 'Shirt Sleeves' is growing in front of the somewhat-faded parent leaf.

healthy looking, and succulent — close to the base of the plant. Slice the leaf crossways into sections about 2 inches wide, making a straight cut at the top and a sloping cut at the base of each section. Insert the sections to about half their depth in pots of moist growing medium, spaced 1 to 2 inches apart. Make sure you keep the sections right-side up, with the bases pointing down. (They won't root if stuck upside down.) Lightly firm the medium around the cuttings, and water gently.

When propagating begonias, you can use the whole leaf at once. Using a sharp, clean knife, cut a suitable leaf from the plant, then cut off the leaf stalk. Turn the leaf over and make one or two cuts through each of the main veins on the underside. Turn the leaf right-side up again, and lay it on a pot of moist grow- ing medium. Bend a few pieces of wire into a U shape, and use them to pin the leaf to the medium. An alternate technique is to cut the leaf into triangular sec- tions, each containing a piece of main vein. Insert these cuttings, point down, about halfway into moist medium.

Cuttings from Leaf Sections

Cut a fully expanded green leaf from the base of the parent plant with a sharp knife. Slice the leaf into 2-inch sections, making a straight cut at the top and a sloping cut at the base of each section. Insert cuttings halfway into moist growing medium.

For other plants, cut the leaf off the parent plant with 1 to 2 inches of stem, or right at the leaf base if the leaf grows directly from the stem. Insert the leaf stem, or the bottom third of a stemless leaf, into moist growing medium. Lightly firm the medium around the cuttings, and water gently.

Cuttings from Begonia Leaves

Using a sharp knife, cut a fully expanded leaf from the plant, then cut off the leaf stalk.
Turn the leaf over and make a 1-inch-long cut through each of the main veins on the underside.
Turn the leaf right-side up again, and lay it on a pot of moist growing medium, pinning it to the top of the pot with a few pieces of wire bent into a U shape.

Cuttings from African Violet Leaves

Use a sharp knife to cut off one leaf with 1 to 2 inches of stem. Insert the stem, up to the base of the leaf, in a guide hole you've made with a pencil. Firm the medium lightly to hold the leaf in place.

Caring for Leaf Cuttings

Immediately after planting, set your potted leaf cuttings in their enclosure (a commercial propagator, a clear plastic sweater box, or a homemade plastic-covered frame) and cover them to minimize moisture loss from the leaves. Place the enclosed cuttings in a warm spot (about 65° to 70°F air temperature). Setting them on a heated propagation mat to keep the medium at 70° to 75°F will hasten rooting. Give your leaf cuttings as much light as possible, but never set them in direct sunlight, which can overheat the air in their enclosure and kill them. Then follow the care guidelines given in "Caring for Soft-Stemmed Cuttings" on page 81.

Within a few weeks, your leaf cuttings should start to produce roots, and then new top growth. Separate the cuttings and plant them in individual 3- to 4-inch pots, as you would annual or perennial cuttings.

TROUBLESHOOTING: *Leaf Cuttings*

PROBLEM: Cuttings wilt.

Cause	Solution
Air too dry around cuttings.	Enclose potted cuttings in a commercial propagator, clear plastic sweater box, or homemade plastic frame to keep humidity high; mist with a hand sprayer if needed. Water before growing medium dries out.
Temperature too hot.	Set covered cuttings where they'll get plenty of light but no direct sun.
Leaves too young.	Try again with a more mature leaf.

PROBLEM: Cuttings rot.

Cause	Solution
Medium too wet.	Use containers with drainage holes, and don't allow water to collect in the flat the pots are sitting in. Water sparingly.
Medium contaminated.	Try again with fresh growing medium; do not reuse medium for planting more cuttings. Remove dead cuttings as soon as you see them. Water with fresh tap water, not water that's been stored outdoors.

PROBLEM: Cuttings do not root.

Cause	Solution
Temperature too hot or cool.	Keep air temperature between 65° and 70°F and the medium at 70° to 75°F; use a heating mat if necessary.

PROBLEM: Cuttings die soon after potting.

Cause	Solution
Insufficient root system.	Leave in cutting pot a week or so longer next time to allow better root development.
Lack of nutrients.	A week or so after transplanting, start fertilizing with a liquid fertilizer, following the directions on the label.

CUTTINGS FROM ROOTS

With most cuttings, you are encouraging leaves or shoots to produce roots. But in some cases, you can also get roots to produce both leafy growth and a new root system. Root cuttings are an easy and reliable way to reproduce a number of perennials, shrubs, vines, and trees. In fact, you may use this technique unintentionally when you dig up certain perennials, such as purple coneflower *(Echinacea purpurea)*. Within a few weeks or months after transplanting the parent plants, you may find new plants sprouting up from the roots you left in the original location.

Late winter to early spring is generally the best time to gather root cuttings, when the soil has thawed and dried out enough to dig. (In mild-winter areas, you can take root cuttings as early as December.) At this time, the roots are full

---

BEST BETS: *Root Cuttings*

Here's an overview of some of the easiest plants to grow from root cuttings. Start with these, then experiment with others to see which will work for you. Keep in mind that root cuttings from most variegated plants, such as 'Harlequin' and 'Nora Leigh' phlox (both cultivars of *Phlox paniculata*), will produce all-green plants; propagate these by division or cuttings instead.

Perennials
Acanthus spp. Bear's breeches.
Anemone × hybrida. Japanese anemone.
Dicentra spectabilis. Bleeding-heart.
Echinacea purpurea. Purple coneflower.
Echinops spp. Globe thistles.
Eryngium spp. Sea hollies.
Geranium spp. Hardy geraniums.
Macleaya cordata. Plume poppy.
Papaver orientale. Oriental poppy.
Phlox paniculata. Garden phlox.
Primula denticulata. Drumstick primrose.
Verbascum spp. Mulleins.

Shrubs, Vines, and Trees
Campsis radicans. Trumpet vine.
Koelreuteria paniculata. Golden rain tree.
Paulownia tomentosa. Princess tree.
Rhus spp. Sumacs.
Robinia pseudoacacia. Black locust.
Sophora japonica. Japanese pagoda tree.

Cuttings from Thin Roots

Dig up the plant, rinse the soil off the roots, and use scissors to cut off a few whole roots close to the crown. Snip the roots into 2-inch sections, and lay them about 1 inch apart on the surface of the moist growing medium. Cover the roots with another ½ inch of medium. Replant the parent clump.

of stored food, and new growth has not yet begun. Plus, the plant you are taking cuttings from will have time to recover from the disturbance and grow normally in the spring. Two exceptions to cold-season cutting collection are Oriental poppies *(Papaver orientale)* and bleeding-hearts *(Dicentra* spp.). Gather cuttings from these plants in midsummer, a few weeks after flowering.

Gathering and Planting Root Cuttings

With small plants, such as drumstick primroses *(Primula denticulata),* you can dig up the whole plant, rinse the soil off the roots, take your cuttings, and

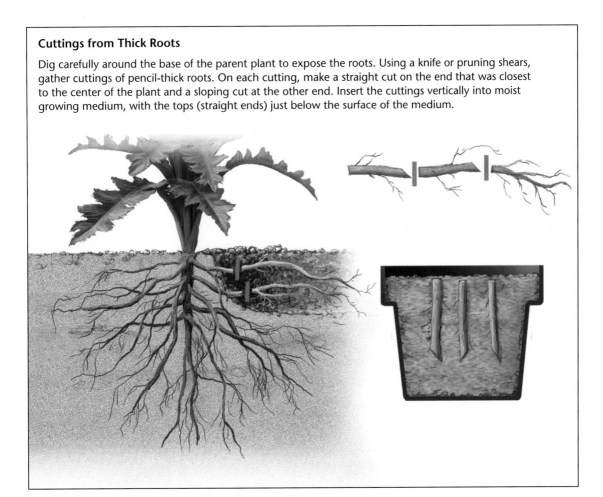

Cuttings from Thick Roots

Dig carefully around the base of the parent plant to expose the roots. Using a knife or pruning shears, gather cuttings of pencil-thick roots. On each cutting, make a straight cut on the end that was closest to the center of the plant and a sloping cut at the other end. Insert the cuttings vertically into moist growing medium, with the tops (straight ends) just below the surface of the medium.

TROUBLESHOOTING: *Root Cuttings*

PROBLEM: Cuttings rot.

Cause	Solution
Medium too wet.	Avoid overwatering. Do not allow pots to sit in water.
Medium contaminated.	Do not reuse growing medium; try again with fresh medium. Water with fresh tap water, not with water that's been stored outdoors.

PROBLEM: Cuttings die soon after transplanting.

Cause	Solution
Transplanted too soon.	Wait until roots are visible in the bottom of the pots before transplanting.
Lack of nutrients.	A week or so after transplanting, start fertilizing with a liquid fertilizer, following the directions on the label.

---

replant. With larger plants, you're better off digging carefully around the base of the plant to expose the roots, taking your cuttings, and replacing the soil. Place gathered cuttings in a plastic bag to keep them from drying out until you are ready to prepare and plant them.

For plants with relatively fine roots, such as garden phlox *(Phlox paniculata),* cut off whole roots with clean, sharp scissors or garden shears, then snip them into 2-inch sections. Where the roots are thick or fleshy, select pencil-thick roots and gather 2- to 3-inch long sections with a clean, sharp knife or pruning shears. Like stem cuttings, root cuttings must be planted right-side up; unlike stem cuttings, the entire root cutting goes underground. To keep track of which is which, on each thick or fleshy cutting, make a straight cut on the end that was closest to the center of the plant, and a sloping cut at the other end. It's best to take no more than about five roots from any plant, or it may not recover.

Most root cuttings don't need heat to do well, so you can simply plant them in pots and set them in a cold frame or a cool, bright room. Gather some 4-inch plastic pots, and a flat or two to carry them in. You'll also need some kind of growing medium; a mix of equal parts peat moss and perlite works well. Moisten the mix and fill the pots — to within 1/2 inch of the rim for thick or fleshy cuttings, or 3/4 inch below the rim for thin cuttings. If your space for pots is limited, cuttings from shrubs, vines, and trees can be tough enough to withstand planting directly outdoors in a well-drained nursery bed; simply loosen the soil a bit and smooth the surface before planting.

Lay thin-rooted cuttings horizontally on the surface of the mix, spaced about 1 inch apart, and cover them with an additional 1/2 inch of mix. Insert thicker cuttings vertically into the mix or soil, with the flat end of the cutting pointing upward. Space them about 2 inches apart, with the tops even with or just below the surface. Water thoroughly to settle the medium around the roots.

Aftercare

While they are rooting indoors or outside, keep your root cuttings evenly moist, but not wet. Root cuttings often produce top growth before their new roots are established. Wait until you can see roots through the pot's drainage holes before transplanting to individual pots or to a nursery bed. Transplant the young plants to the garden in the fall, if they are large enough, or leave them in a cold frame or nursery bed for an extra growing season, if needed.

CHAPTER 5
LAYERING ESTABLISHED PLANTS

Layering is the technique of encouraging plant stems to root while they are still attached to the parent plant. Some plants, such as strawberries and shrubby dogwoods (*Cornus* spp.) layer themselves naturally, sending out stems that creep along the soil surface and take root, producing new shoots from the rooting points. You can propagate these productive plants easily by simply severing the rooted shoots and digging them up. (See "Removing Offsets, Runners, and Suckers" on page 58 for details on care.) But you don't have to wait for the plants to layer themselves: a few simple steps will help you speed up the process.

As with cuttings and division, layering will give you an exact copy of the parent plant. You generally won't get as many new plants as you would by taking cuttings: since layering takes up some garden space, you'll usually layer only one or two branches at a time. But it's an excellent way to root almost any woody plant, especially those that normally don't root dependably from cuttings.

You can start layers just about any time, but you'll get the fastest results by preparing them in late winter to early spring, just before new growth starts.

Air layering is a simple, effective technique for propagating a variety of houseplants. Roots form in the sphagnum moss held in place and kept moist by a piece of plastic wrapped around the stem.

Layering a Runner

You can encourage runners to root by pinning them into a pot of moist growing medium while they are still attached to their parent.

SIMPLE LAYERING

Simple layering involves bending a branch down to the ground and encouraging roots to form where it touches the soil. It's easy to do, as long as the plant you want to propagate has somewhat flexible stems that are fairly close to the ground. If not, air layering, discussed on page 109, may be a good option.

Preparing the Layer

Simple layering requires no special equipment: just a trowel or spade to loosen the soil and some wire pins, bricks, or rocks to help hold the stem to the soil. You may also need a knife to nick the stem, and a stake to support the stem tip.

In late winter to early spring, select a low, flexible shoot from the plant you want to propagate. Carefully bend the shoot to the ground. It should touch the ground at one point, at least — somewhere between 6 and 18 inches or so behind the stem tip — with minimal help from you. Mark the point on the ground where the shoot easily touches the soil. Allow the stem to come back up, holding it with your fingers close to the point where it touched the ground. Pull or cut off any leaves 3 to 4 inches on either side of that point. Using a sharp, clean

Preparing a Simple Layer

Bend a young, flexible stem near the base of a shrub to the ground, and set a rock on the soil to mark a spot roughly 1 foot behind the stem tip. Remove the leaves where the stem touches the ground, and use a knife to slice a sliver of bark off the underside of the stem. Loosen the soil in the spot you marked on the ground, and bend the stem to the ground again. Bury the wounded section about 3 inches deep, using a wire pin if needed to hold the stem in place, and tie the shoot tip to a stake to encourage upright growth.

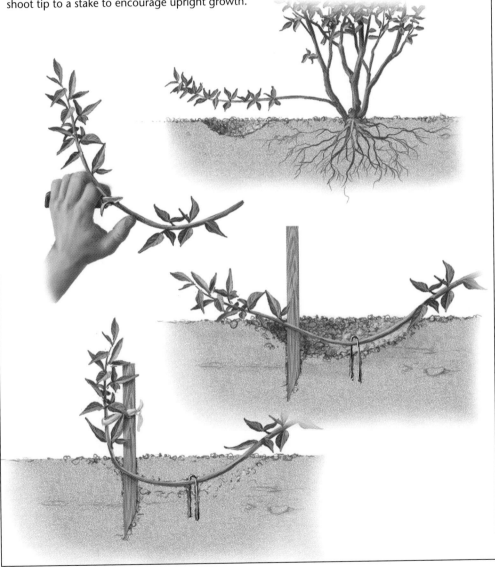

BEST BETS: *Simple Layering*

Simple layering is a great way to propagate a wide variety of woody plants. You can try this technique with just about any plant with a stem that you can bend to the ground. A few of the easiest plants to layer are listed below, but feel free to experiment with your own shrubs, trees, and vines.

Camellia spp. Camellias.

Clematis spp. and hybrids. Clematis.

Cornus spp. Shrubby dogwoods.

Cotoneaster spp. Cotoneasters.

Hedera spp. Ivies.

Hydrangea spp. Hydrangeas.

Ilex spp. Hollies.

Jasminum spp. Jasmines.

Kalmia spp. Mountain laurels.

Ligustrum spp. Privets.

Lonicera spp. Honeysuckles.

Magnolia spp. Magnolias.

Pieris spp. Pieris.

Pyracantha spp. Firethorns.

Rhododendron spp. Azaleas and rhododendrons.

Rosa spp. and hybrids. Roses.

Syringa spp. Lilacs.

Viburnum spp. Viburnums.

Vitis spp. Grapes.

Weigela spp. Weigelas.

Wisteria spp. Wisterias.

knife, also cut a thin sliver of bark (1 to 2 inches long) off the bottom side of the stem a few inches up from that point to encourage rooting.

Next, loosen the soil about 5 inches deep in a circle 4 to 6 inches wide around the point where the stem touched the ground. Bend the stem back down, and bury the wounded section about 3 inches deep in the center of the loosened area, pinning it down with a U-shaped wire pin, if needed. Insert a stake into the soil next to the exposed shoot tip, and tie the shoot to the stake with yarn or soft string to encourage upright growth. You may also need to set a brick or rock on the buried section to help hold it down.

If you choose to layer a very flexible shoot that will easily lay flat against the soil, you can layer the whole stem. Loosen the top 4 inches or so of soil where the shoot will contact the soil, then pin the stem to the soil with several U-shaped wire pins, or hold it in place with one or two bricks or rocks. Cover the stem with 1 to 2 inches of sandy soil, compost, or mulch.

Aftercare

After preparing a layer, water the soil thoroughly. Over the next few months, water as needed during dry spells to keep the soil evenly moist; otherwise, leave

---

TROUBLESHOOTING: *Simple Layering*

PROBLEM: Layer does not form roots by the end of the first growing season.

Cause	Solution
Plant is naturally slow to root.	Leave the layer in place for another year or two, until roots develop and get established. Dusting the wounded part of the stem with rooting hormone before burying it may speed up rooting next time.
Soil is dry.	Water regularly to keep the soil around the layer evenly moist; mulching around the layer will also help.

PROBLEM: Layer dies soon after transplanting.

Cause	Solution
Insufficient root system.	Next time, leave the stem attached to the parent plant for an additional year to make sure the roots are well established before transplanting.

---

the layer undisturbed. In fall, you can test for rooting. Remove any bricks, rocks, or pins holding the stem to the ground, and tug lightly on the upright growth. If the growth feels loose, leave the layer in place for another year. If there is some resistance, carefully dig down to check the progress of the roots. If there are just a few small roots, replace the soil and leave the layer in place until the following spring or fall. When there are multiple sturdy-looking roots, sever the stem from its parent. (If you pinned the whole stem to the ground, you will likely have several rooted shoots; cut them apart and handle them as individual plants.) Transplant the rooted layer to another spot in the garden, and care for it as you would any new plant.

AIR LAYERING

With air layering, you take the soil to the stem, instead of the stem to the soil. This technique usually works best when started in spring on stems of the previous year's growth, but you can use older stems if necessary. One-year-old shoots usually have greenish or light brown stems; older growth is generally darker brown or gray.

BEST BETS: *Air Layering*

Air layering works well on a wide variety of hardy shrubs and trees, including all those listed in "Best Bets: Simple Layering" on page 108. It's also a great way to propagate many tropical and subtropical shrubs and trees, including those grown as houseplants; a few of the best candidates are listed here.

Citrus spp. Lemons, oranges, and other citrus.
Codiaeum spp. Crotons.
Cordyline spp. Cordylines.
Dieffenbachia spp. Dumb canes.
Dracaena spp. Dracaenas.
Ficus spp. Figs.
Philodendron spp. Philodendrons.

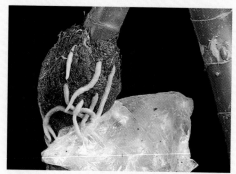

Roots on stem of air-layered Dieffenbachia

Preparing the Layer

When you are ready to start a layer, gather your materials. You'll need a piece of plastic wrap about 8 inches square. For outdoor layers, it's helpful to have an 8-inch-square piece of black plastic or aluminum foil as well. You'll also need a sharp, clean knife, some adhesive tape (such as electrician's tape), rooting hormone powder, a small brush to apply the powder, and some sphagnum moss. (Sphagnum moss is the type with long, stringy fibers, not finely chopped peat moss.) An hour or so before starting a layer, add roughly two handfuls of the sphagnum moss to a bowl of warm water, and allow it to soak.

Use a sharp, clean knife to wound the stem some distance back from the stem tip, but within the previous season's growth: a point roughly 6 to 12 inches back from the tip, depending on the plant's vigor. You may girdle the stem, removing a ring about 1/2 inch wide all around the stem, or make a shallow, 1- to 2-inch-long, upward-slanting cut through the bark on one side of the stem. If you choose the latter approach, insert a toothpick or a bit of moist sphagnum moss into the "tongue" to keep the cut surfaces from growing back together. With a small paintbrush, dust all cut surfaces with rooting hormone.

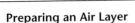

Preparing an Air Layer

Make an upward-slanting cut about halfway through the stem to make a "tongue," and tuck a wad of moist sphagnum moss under it to hold it open. Wrap the bottom edge of a square of plastic wrap around the stem and secure it with tape. Wad two handfuls of moist sphagnum moss around the stem and the wounded area. Bring the free end of the plastic up to enclose the moss, and secure the upper side of the plastic around the stem with tape. When roots are visible in the moss, cut below the bottom of the plastic. Remove the wrapping and excess moss, then plant in a pot or nursery bed.

Take the piece of plastic wrap, wrap one side around the stem 2 to 3 inches below the wounded area, and tape it to the stem. Fold out the free end of the plastic to expose the wounded area again. Take two handfuls of the soaked sphagnum moss, squeeze them to remove excess moisture, and wad them around the wounded area of the stem. Hold the moss in place with one hand, while you bring the free end of the plastic up again and wrap it around the moss. When you get the moss completely enclosed in the plastic, securely tape the free end of the plastic wrap to the stem above the wounded area. It's important to make sure the moss doesn't dry out during the rooting, so on outdoor layers, it may help to cover the wrapped area with a piece of aluminum foil or an extra piece of plastic wrap.

Aftercare

Check on the layer every few weeks, removing the outer wrapping if there is one. If it looks like the moss is drying out, open the plastic, moisten the moss with water from a spray bottle, and rewrap the area. Otherwise, just leave the plastic

TROUBLESHOOTING: *Air Layering*

PROBLEM: Layer does not root by end of first growing season.

Cause	Solution
Needs more time.	Some plants are naturally slow to produce roots, especially from older stems; leave the layer in place for another growing season.
Moss dried out.	Check layer every few weeks and moisten moss, if needed. If moss has gotten completely dry, start over with a new cut and moistened moss.
Moss is too wet.	Squeeze moss to remove excess water before wrapping it around stem. Tape upper end of wrapping closely so that rainwater can't enter.

PROBLEM: Layer roots by end of first season but dies the next spring.

Cause	Solution
Developing roots killed by cold.	Try again the following spring, starting with young, quicker-rooting growth. If there are any roots by fall, cut the layer off the parent, plant it in a pot of moist growing mix, and set it in a cold frame for the winter to allow the roots a chance to develop.

wrap in place. Eventually, by the end of one or two growing seasons, you will be able to see developing roots through the plastic.

On indoor plants, you can remove rooted layers at any time. Simply cut them free of the parent plant, remove the plastic and excess moss, and transplant to individual pots of moist growing mix. Wait until the dormant season (fall or early spring) to sever rooted layers from outdoor plants. It's usually best to plant these layers in a nursery bed or a pot of moist growing mix and allow them to grow for a year or so before moving them to the garden.

MOUND LAYERING

Mound layering is a good way to get several new plants from one shrub. It's especially handy for renewing shrubby herbs, which tend to get sparse and woody-stemmed after a few years. But you can also buy a new plant particularly for this technique. If you'd like a ground cover of heather, for instance, you could buy one or two plants, mound layer them, and have many young rooted plants in a year or two.

Preparing the Layer

Spring is a good time to prepare a mound layer. All you need is a small bucketful of loose, sandy soil or finely shredded bark mulch — ideally mixed with a handful or two of compost. Once the stems have rooted, you'll need pruning shears to

---

BEST BETS: *Mound Layering*

These plants respond well to mound layering. Feel free to experiment with other shrubby plants as well!

Artemisia spp. Artemisias, including southernwood and wormwood.
Calluna vulgaris. Heather.
Erica spp. Heaths.
Hyssopus officinalis. Hyssop.

Lavandula spp. Lavenders.
Salvia officinalis. Sage.
Santolina spp. Lavender cottons.
Satureja montana. Winter savory.
Thymus spp. Thymes.

sever them from the parent plant. You can pot them up in 4-inch pots of moist growing mix, plant them in a nursery bed, or plant them directly in the garden.

To layer an established plant, mound roughly 3 to 5 inches of crumbly, sandy soil or mulch over the center of the plant, leaving 3 to 4 inches of each shoot tip exposed. Work the soil or mulch around the stems with your fingers to eliminate air pockets. Water carefully just after mounding (a strong spray of water will wash away the soil or mulch).

If you've purchased a plant just for mound layering, plant it in a nursery bed,

Preparing a Mound Layer

Mound several inches of sandy soil or mulch over the base of the plant. Work the mulch around the stems with your fingers, leaving only a few inches of each shoot tip exposed. After several months, pull away the mounded soil or mulch, and snip off the rooted stems.

TROUBLESHOOTING: *Mound Layering*

PROBLEM: **Stems do not root by end of first growing season.**

Cause	Solution
Plant is naturally slow to root.	Young stems usually root quickly; older, woody growth may take longer. Leave the mound in place for another 6 to 12 months.
Mound dried out or washed away.	Water during dry spells to keep the mound moist. If rain washes the mound away, replace soil or mulch to keep the stem bases covered.

---

setting it about 2 inches deeper than it was growing in its container. Mound a few extra inches of soil or mulch around the stems, if needed, as described for an established plant.

Aftercare

Over the next few months, water again as needed during dry spells to keep the mound from drying out. If heavy rains wash part of the mound away, add more soil or mulch. In late summer to early fall, pull away some of the soil or mulch with your fingers to see if roots have formed along the covered parts of the stems. If there are few or no roots, leave the mound in place and check again in spring.

When the roots look sturdy and are prolific, pull away more of the mound, and snip off the rooted stems near the original soil level, keeping as many roots as possible on each piece. If you have a planting site prepared and the stems are well rooted, you can plant them directly in the garden. Otherwise, plant the rooted stems in individual pots of moist growing mix, or in a nursery bed, and allow them to grow there until the following spring or fall; then transplant them to the garden.

In some cases, the original plant may produce new growth from the roots after this process. If it isn't growing in a highly visible spot, you may want to leave it in place for a season after removing the mound to see if it sprouts again. Otherwise, just dig it out, work a few handfuls of compost into the site, and replant with one or more of the rooted stems.

PHOTO CREDITS

David Cavagnaro: 20, 50, 75

Barbara Ellis: iii, 2

Derek Fell: vi–1

Charles Marden Fitch: 66, 72, 94, 104, 110

Nancy J. Ondra: 37, 39

Jerry Pavia: 17

INDEX

Page numbers in italics refer to illustrations.

Titles available in the Taylor's Weekend Gardening Guides series:

Organic Pest and Disease Control	$12.95
Safe and Easy Lawn Care	12.95
Window Boxes	12.95
Attracting Birds and Butterflies	12.95
Water Gardens	12.95
Easy, Practical Pruning	12.95
The Winter Garden	12.95
Backyard Building Projects	12.95
Indoor Gardens	12.95
Plants for Problem Places	12.95
Soil and Composting	12.95
Kitchen Gardens	12.95
Garden Paths	12.95
Easy Plant Propagation	12.95

At your bookstore or by calling 1-800-225-3362

Prices subject to change without notice